Revelations of the New Lemuria

Aurelia Louise Jones

Mount Shasta Light Publishing

TELOS - Volume 1
Revelations of the New Lemuria

ISBN 978-0-9700902-4-9

© Copyright 2004 by Aurelia Louise Jones
English Publication - May 2004
Second Printing - April 2006
Third Printing - April 2008
Fourth Printing - July 2009

Mount Shasta Light Publishing
PO Box 1509
Mount Shasta CA 96067-1509 – USA

Phone: 530-926-4599
Fax: 530-926-4159

E-mail: aurelia@mslpublishing.com
Web Site: www.mslpublishing.com
Also: www.lemurianconnection.com

Cover Photography: Erich Ziller
Cover Design: Aaron Rose
Page Layout and Formatting: Aaron Rose

It is with much delight, joy and anticipation that we bring to you the memories of Lemuria. Though these memories have appeared lost for awhile, they have continued to live and thrive in your hearts unto this now moment in time. In Telos, we are honored to join hearts with you to assist in the unification of our two civilizations.

We send you much love from Telos, where this divine energy flows in great abundance. Until we meet, keep practicing the art of true love, which begins with loving yourself. May love abound in your hearts for each other and for all of creation, as precious jewels and expressions of the Love of our Mother/Father God! We hold you dearly in our hearts.

- Adama, Galatia and Ahnahmar

Table of Contents

Dedication vi
Acknowledgements vii
A Word from Aurelia Louise Jones viii
Welcome From Adama xi

Part One
Our Lemurian Connection

1. **About Mount Shasta, Telos and Lemuria**
   "The Magic Mountain" - *Aurelia* 3
2. **Lemuria - Her Origin** - *Adama* 11
   Opening to the Heart of Lemuria - *Aurelia* 13
   Healing the Heart of Lemuria - *Adama* 19
3. **The New Lemuria** - *Adama* 23
   As Earth Beings, We Are One Big Family 26

Part Two
Messages from Adama, High Priest of Telos

4. **Government of Telos** 33
   The City of Telos 34
   Transportation in Telos 35
   Physical Appearance of the Telosians 36
   Celebration of Holidays 36
   We Live in Circular Homes 38
   Tunnels Inside the Earth 41
   Shamballa and Her Role 42
   Inhabitants of the Earth's Interior 42
   Other Cities of the Agartha Network 43
5. **Emergence Update** 45
6. **Telos Codes of Entry** 51
7. **The Children of Telos** 55
   The Future of Our Children 56
   Growing Up in Telos 57

8. **Temple of Union**..61
   Marriages in Telos..66
   Relationships and Sexuality in Telos..........................69
   The Bringing Forth of Children..................................75

9. **The Animals in Telos**..81

10. **Questions and Answers**
    Interventions from Other Races..................................87
    Crop Circles..89
    Crystals..90
    Guardians of Portals and Gateways............................92

11. **We Have Immortalized Our Bodies**......................97
    Your Physical Body Mirrors Your Consciousness........99
    How to Raise One's Consciousness............................104

12. **Come Home, Beloved Ones, Come Home!**
    The Fifth Dimension is Awaiting Your Return!.111
    Hold Peace and Love in Your Hearts - *Galatia*..........120

13. **The Great Jade Lemurian Temple of Telos &**
    The Flame of Healing, A Fifth Ray Activity.........125
    Conscious Meditation to the Great Jade Temple.......138

Part Three
Messages from Various Beings

14. **Messages from El Morya**
    The Consciousness that Functions on "Automatic
    Pilot" is Not Heading for the Ascension Door..........145
    The Christing of Our Planet Has Begun...................149

15. **Wake-Up Call from the Redwood Trees**.............153

16. **Telos, A Living Library** - *Thomas*.......................161

17. **Final Words from Adama**....................................165

    Regarding Channeling Adama..................................168
    Note from Aurelia Louise Jones...............................173
    Mount Shasta Light Publishing Publications............175
    Telos and Lemurian Connection Associations...........176

Dedication

I would like to dedicate this book to all the ascended beings who are helping humanity and the ascension of this planet from the other side of the veil; especially Lord Maitreya, Lord Sananda, Saint Germain, El Morya, Quan Yin, Mother Mary, Kuthumi and Archangel Michael. I want to acknowledge Mother Earth for her infinite love and patience in providing a platform for the evolution of our souls in gaining greater wisdom and understanding. I also want to express my deep love and gratitude to Adama, the high priest of Telos, who has been so loving and patient with me, and to all my Lemurian family of Telos.

Acknowledgements

To my sister Helen, to my brother Guy and their families who have always been so close to me in this life, always ready to extend love, understanding and a helping hand. To Thomas, my former brother in the time of Lemuria, and to my parents who are now assisting me from the other side of the veil! To all members of the Telos World-Wide Foundation, who are working with so much love and dedication to assist the emergence of our Lemurian family.

I want to express my deep gratitude to our Lemurian brothers and sisters who have held the energies of the Ascension Flame for the planet until we become spiritually mature enough to hold these energies ourselves.

Last but not least, I wish to honor my beloved twin flames, Adama and Ahnahmar, who have remained in Telos since our physical separation at the time of the sinking of Lemuria, for patiently awaiting my return. Adama and Ahnahmar, I know that from your realm, you have loved and supported me consistently throughout my long journey on the surface. With deep love, I thank you both with all the gratitude my heart can express.

A Word from Aurelia Louise Jones

A few years ago while I was living in Montana, Lord Sananda *(formerly known in his last incarnation on Earth as the master Jesus)* told me in a channeling session that I would eventually move to the Mount Shasta area to prepare for a much greater arena of service in fulfillment to humanity and the planet.

A few months later, in February of 1997, I received an e-mail message on my computer from Adama, the high priest of Telos, inviting me to consider moving to the Mount Shasta area to prepare for an eventual mission with the Lemurians. The message was not very long, about 12 to 15 lines, but very specific. It carried a wonderful love energy vibration. I was quite surprised, to say the least, and was excited about receiving such a message from those I had been hoping to reconnect with for so long. I soon began to make my plans to move to Mount Shasta, and I arrived with all my belongings and family of cats one year later in June of 1998.

Three years after my move, to my disappointment and sadness, I felt that I had gone through a long series of intense initiations but still had not received any contact or communication from the Lemurians. I began to think they were ignoring me or I was not "good enough." Perhaps they had changed their minds about working with me, or I had failed their tests. I was unaware that all this time I had been receiving a long series of what is known as "the initiations of the mountain" and was being prepared on the inner plane for my mission of service.

Finally, one afternoon, totally unexpectedly, I received a letter from Adama, hand-delivered by a messenger. The letter informed me I was now ready to start working more closely and consciously with him in fulfilling my mission. I then received another series of intense initiations, some regarding my channeling skills, which up to that point I had been hesitant to explore.

In another communication from Lord Sananda a few months later, I was told that the time for Adama to be heard on this planet had come, and that he had chosen to work through me for this very purpose. He also shared what an awesome ascended master Adama was, and added: "Know this, Adama does not do anything in a small way. He has big plans. He intends to be heard in a big way on this planet. Prepare yourself for this deep merging of his energies with yours and the unfolding of his plan."

At that point, I was a beginner at channeling. I knew I had to go beyond my fears, self-doubts and hesitation rather quickly and purposefully to sharpen my channeling skills. There was no more time for me to sit on top of hills and watch the clouds go by. Almost immediately, and in spite of myself, several people started asking me to channel written material from Adama for them or to have private channeled sessions with him. I was invited to channel Adama for various public presentations. Since then, I have channeled him several times in small and large public events in the U.S., Canada, France, Switzerland and Belgium.

It is obvious to me now that this was only the beginning, and that my mission with the Lemurians was unfolding and expanding into a much greater arena of service. Opportunities were opening rapidly, and basically all I needed to do was to make myself available for service. I greatly enjoyed bringing through the new information for these books and there will be much more to come in the future. Each time I channel Adama, I feel him directly within my heart. I feel warmth and comfort from his love that expands and glows. When I feel his energy within my heart, it makes my heart sing. I now know him as a most loving, trustworthy and loyal friend.

When more direct contact with the Telosians had manifested, I also connected closely with other wondrous beings from Telos. I reconnected with former Lemurian family members, including a conscious connection with my twin flame Ahnahmar, who has been living in Telos in the same physical body since the demise of Lemuria. As I walk and explore various areas around Mount Shasta, my "Lemurian team," as they call themselves, always seems to be with me. They have shown me several ancient sacred sites and temples that still exist in the fifth dimension. We've visited entrances to multi-dimensional corridors and portals, energy vortexes, fairy lands, and even a place where large families of unicorns still live. They reside in a dimension that is slightly above ours and are visible only to those with expanded inner vision.

The places they have shown me have not yet been recognized or unveiled by anyone on the surface, and they must remain veiled until the right vibration prevails on our planet. I also know that there is much more to be discovered on the surface and inside the Earth than we could possibly imagine, and it will gradually be disclosed as a progressive revelation.

This is exciting, my friends, because as we open our consciousness to our divinity, as we let go of duality to embrace harmlessness and oneness, a new world will emerge right in front of our eyes. This world waits upon our awakening to a reality that has always existed, a reality that was only veiled from our sight by our long journey into the illusion of separation from God. This world is filled with magic, love, wonders and great diversity. How exciting it will be for all of us to rediscover the treasures we left behind a very long time ago.

The return of the Lemurians and their eventual emergence among us is nothing less than the "Second Coming" that has long been awaited. Long ago, the Lemurians achieved the fullness of Christ consciousness. When we are ready to receive them among us, they will teach us how to implement, right here on the surface of this planet, the type of paradise they have forged for themselves in Telos. They will assist us in birthing a golden age that will manifest the fullness of the Christ consciousness, which is the divinity that has always resided within our hearts. The indwelling Christ of our being will become tangibly manifest on this planet and in our daily lives.

Welcome From Adama

Greetings, my dear friends,

It is indeed with great joy and excitement in our hearts that we of Telos connect, in the energy of love, with all of you who feel drawn to the Revelations of the New Lemuria.

On behalf of the Lemurian Council of Twelve of Telos, the king and queen of Telos, Ra and Rana Mu, and all of your former brothers and sisters of the present-day Lemurian civilization, we welcome you to the Heart of Lemuria, the Heart of Compassion. We are indeed the survivors of that mighty civilization, and to the great surprise of many on the surface, we reveal to you at this important time in Earth's evolution, that we are real, very well and alive within Mount Shasta, California, after 12,000 years of isolation from the surface population.

The time has now come, beloved ones, for our two civilizations to reunite again. One of the main purposes of our writings is to assist in the establishment of the foundation necessary to prepare for our eventual emergence among you. The long dark night that has separated us for so long is now over. We are planning to emerge among you in the near future to reunite in love, wisdom and understanding with those of you who are ready.

It is our heart-felt desire to teach you what we have learned since the sinking of the Lemurian continent, and to assist you in creating for yourselves the type of paradise we have created for ourselves. We have forged the path for you, and when we share this higher level of spiritual wisdom and understanding, it will be much easier for you to follow in our footsteps. We will walk side-by side with you along the way.

It is especially heart-warming for us to see our information published in several languages, because we are aware that it will reach a much greater population on the planet. Many souls in other countries are ready and yearning to reconnect with us and with the aspect of themselves which lived on the Lemurian continent. So many of you who are drawn to this material have, to this day, former family members living in Telos or in present-day Lemuria. These family members and friends love you so very much and are longing to reconnect with you. Many of our people in Telos, who have former family members living on the surface, have learned your language in order to communicate with you with ease at the time of our emergence.

We ask you, dear ones, to take our information to heart and make a conscious effort to create a bridge of love and communication between our two civilizations. It is that bridge of love and receptivity from your hearts to ours that will bring us to you in a more tangible way. We are awaiting your response. Call on us in your hearts, and we will be at your side, whispering and singing to you our "song of union and oneness." We all champion your victory. We are always available to assist you in reaching your goals and hearts' desires.

I am Adama, your Lemurian brother.

Adama
High Priest of Telos

Part One

Our Lemurian Connection

To return to full consciousness,
As divine beings,
It is imperative that you now begin
To turn the leadership over
To the heart,
And allow the heart to rule again,
Rather than the mind.
- Ahnahmar

Chapter One

About Mount Shasta, Telos and Lemuria

"The Magic Mountain" - by Aurelia

Mount Shasta is a most majestic mountain that anchors the northern end of the Sierra Nevada Mountain range. It is located in Siskiyou County in Northern California, approximately 40 miles from the Oregon border. Mount Shasta is the cone of an extinct volcano rising to a height of 14,162 feet above sea level, and is the largest volcanic peak in the continental United States. The ascended masters have revealed that Mount Shasta can also be considered an embodiment of the Great Central Sun.

Mount Shasta, more than just a mountain, is one of the most sacred places on the planet. It is a mystical power source for this Earth and a focus for a City of Light, for angels, spirit-guides, spaceships and ascended masters from the Light Realm and many dimensions. Mount Shasta is also the home of the survivors of Ancient Lemuria.

For those gifted with clairvoyant abilities, Mount Shasta is embraced in a gigantic, etheric purple pyramid whose capstone extends far beyond this planet into space, and connects us intergalactically to the Confederation of Planets for this sector of the Milky Way Galaxy. This awesome pyramid also includes an inverted version of itself that extends down

3

to the very core of the Earth. Mount Shasta represents the entry point of the Light-Grids for this planet. It is the location where most of the energy arrives initially from the galactic and universal core before it is disseminated to other mountains and into the rest of the grids. Most mountaintops, especially tall mountains, are Beacons of Light feeding the light-grids of this planet.

Strange lights and sounds are often seen or heard on the mountain. Lenticular clouds, shadows and outstanding sunsets add to its mystical aura and there are many openings and portals into the fifth dimensional cities that still exist from the time of Lemuria. Mount Shasta is the home of many present-day Lemurians who are survivors of the sinking of the continent of Lemuria over 12,000 years ago. Yes, our Lemurian brothers and sisters are real. They are well and physically alive, and living a fifth dimensional existence that is yet invisible to our eyes. The "surface" vibration is currently transitioning from the third dimension into a fourth/fifth dimensional reality. The other dimensions exist around us but most people living on the surface do not yet possess a consciousness evolved enough to perceive them.

Prior to the sinking of their continent, the ancient Lemurians were fully aware of the eventual destiny of their beloved land and used their mastery of energy, crystals, sound and vibrations to hollow out a vast underground city with the intention of preserving their culture, their treasures and their records of ancient Earth history. This section of history has been lost to humanity since the sinking of Atlantis. Lemuria was once a vast continent, larger than North America, connected to parts of California, Oregon, Nevada and Washington states. This large continent disappeared overnight into the Pacific Ocean over 12,000 years ago during a vast cataclysm. All inhabitants of the Earth at that time considered Lemuria their motherland and there was much grieving on the Earth when it was lost.

Approximately 25,000 Lemurians were able to migrate into the interior of Mount Shasta along with the most important of their various administration centers prior to the sinking of the Motherland. Beloveds, you who are reading this now know in your hearts that your former brothers and sisters of Lemuria never left you. They are still here in physical, immortalized bodies, living life in an unlimited fifth dimensional reality.

Native Americans believe that Mount Shasta is a place of such immense grandeur that its existence can only be attributed to the creation of a very "Great Spirit." They also believe that an invisible race of little people, about four feet tall, live along its slopes as Guardians. These wondrous people, often referred to as "The Little People of Mount Shasta," are also physical but of a vibration usually invisible to us. Some of them are occasionally seen in this dimension around the mountain.

The reason they do not show themselves physically to many people is that they have a collective fear of humans. At one time, when they were as visible as we are, humans maligned them. They became so fearful of humans that they asked the spiritual hierarchy of this planet for a dispensation to elevate their frequency. Now they remain invisible and are able to continue their evolution unharmed and in peace.

There are reports of the Bigfoot race being seen on some remote areas of Mount Shasta, along with many other mysterious beings. The Bigfoot people are now very few in number throughout the world and around Mount Shasta. They are of average intelligence and possess a peaceful heart. They have obtained a dispensation that allows for invisibility at will. In this way they are able to avoid confrontation with us and, like the little people, avoid physical harm, mutilation and enslavement in the name of science.

We have not yet, as a species, truly understood that we are invited guests on this planet. We are the guests of our gracious Mother Earth, who has volunteered to provide a platform for the evolution of the many kingdoms that reside here. Humans are only one of those kingdoms. It was firmly intended, and agreed to in the beginning, that all kingdoms would be honored and allowed to share this planet "equally." It was this way for a very long time. Unfortunately, for hundreds of thousands of years, humans have taken over, arrogantly thinking that we are the superior race with the right to control and manipulate other kingdoms.

Many species in the animal kingdom have also become invisible. They are still here but in a slightly higher frequency and thus invisible to us. Where do you think all the supposedly "extinct" species have gone? Many of them are extinct because they have made a collective choice not to interact with us any more. Those animal species which are still physically here are not always loved and honored by us. Go into your heart and explore how most animals are treated, used and abused by this supposedly "superior race."

Today, several spiritual groups live in the Mount Shasta area. Truth seekers who have felt and heard in their hearts the "Call of the Mountain" have moved to this area and feel they have finally "come home." The memory of their far distant Lemurian ancestry is calling them back to a former point of origin.

On a clear day, Mount Shasta stands as a white jewel and can be seen from at least 100 miles away. People who live nearby have remarkable stories about the 14,162-foot volcano. The most remarkable stories are the legends of a mysterious people who live inside the mountain, albeit in a fifth dimensional frequency. They are said to be descendants of an ancient society from the lost continent of Lemuria, living deep inside the mountain in round houses, enjoying unlimited health, wealth and true brotherhood. They have preserved their ancient culture.

The Lemurians living within the mountain are commonly described as graceful beings, seven feet tall or more, with long, flowing hair. They dress at times in white robes and sandals, or in very colorful clothing. They are said to have long, slender necks and bodies which they adorn with beautiful decorative collars made of beads or precious stones. They have evolved their sixth sense, which enables them to communicate among themselves through extra-sensory perception. They can also teleport and make themselves invisible at will. Their mother tongue is the Lemurian language, called Solara Maru, but they also speak an impeccable English with a slight British accent. They have chosen to learn English as a second language because they live in America.

Around 1940, Dr. M. Doreal, claimed that he visited the Lemurians inside their mountain. He said that the space he was shown was about 2 miles high, 20 miles long and 15 miles wide. He wrote that the light inside the mountain was as bright as a summer day and was created by a giant glowing mass of light suspended in the center of that great cavern. Another man reported that he fell asleep on Mount Shasta only to be awakened by a Lemurian who led him inside the mountain to his cave, which was paved with gold. The Lemurian told the man that there were a series of tunnels left by volcanoes that ran under the earth like freeways ... a world within a world.

The Lemurians had reportedly mastered atomic energy, telepathic and clairvoyant skills, electronics and science as much as 18,000 years ago. Most of their technology is controlled through thought. In ancient times, they propelled their boats using energy radiated by crystals. They used airships for travel to Atlantis and other places. Today they have a fleet of spaceships, called the "Silver Fleet," in which they travel to and from the mountain and out into space. They have the ability to render their spaceships invisible and silent to avoid being detected by the local and national military. Although they are physical in nature, they are able to shift their energy fields from third to fourth and fifth dimensional vibration and become visible or invisible at will.

Many people report seeing strange lights on the mountain. One explanation is that there are spacecraft constantly entering and exiting a spaceport deep within the mountain. Mount Shasta is not only a home for the Lemurians, but is also an inter-planetary and inter-galactic multi-dimensional portal. There is a huge etheric City of Light above Mount Shasta called the "Crystal City of the Seven Rays." At some point in our near future, hopefully within the next 12 to 20 years, this wondrous city of Light is destined to be lowered into our physical realm, and become the first City of Light to manifest tangibly on the surface of this planet. In order for this to happen, the people who live here will have to match its vibration in their own consciousness.

You can easily visit the Mount Shasta area without reading or hearing about Lemurians, but if you have some former connections with them, you may be blessed with some revelations. Mount Shasta draws visitors from all over the world, some seeking spiritual insight, others seeking to bask in the beauty and natural wonders that Mother Nature has to offer in this unique alpine region.

Everyone loves a mystery, especially a mystery about Mount Shasta. There have been many fascinating myths and legends written about this Northern California giant. The solitary mountain always slumbers on ... her secrets intact. But every so often, another mysterious story surfaces. New casts of characters emerge and attention is centered once more on the mystic mountain. That's the way it has been for years, and probably always will be. Mount Shasta has a tendency to reveal herself only to those who honor life, themselves for who they truly are, the Earth and all other kingdoms sharing this planet.

Lemuria still exists to this day
In a fifth dimensional frequency,
Not yet visible to your third dimensional
Vision and perception.
- Adama

Chapter Two

Lemuria - Her Origin

Adama

In the beginning, millions of years ago, this planet was created with seven major continents. Almost from the beginning, many colonies of extraterrestrial civilizations came
here to live. Some stayed for short periods, while others
stayed much longer. The details of this past era of Earth's
history are recorded in the library of Porthologos in the
Inner Earth and also in our own Lemurian library in
Telos. Very few, if any, of the true facts of the long history
of this planet still exist on the "surface" today. For most,
those civilizations were not as physical as you experience
yourself today, nor were records kept in the same way.
Nearly all the records that managed to survive the cataclysms on the "surface" were eventually destroyed in one
way or another.

About 4,500,000 years BC, Archangel Michael with his
band of Blue Flame angels and many Beings from the Light
Realm, with the blessing of the Father/Mother God, escorted
to this planet the first souls who were to become the seeds
of the Lemurian race. This took place at the Royal Teton
Retreat, known today as the Grand Teton National Park
near Jackson, Wyoming. These new souls incarnating on
this planet originally came from the Land of Mu in the Dahl

Universe. At that time, the Earth expressed everywhere a perfection, abundance and beauty that can hardly be imagined today. It was indeed the most magnificent paradise of this universe and of the whole of Creation. This perfection was maintained for several million years, until the beginning of the fall in consciousness that took place during the fourth golden age.

Eventually, other races from Sirius, Alpha Centauri, the Pleiades and a few other planets came and joined these "seed" souls to evolve here as well. These races mixed together to form the Lemurian civilization. To say the least, it was quite an awesome mixture! Lemuria, the "Motherland," became the cradle of an enlightened civilization on this planet, assisting in the eventual birth of many other civilizations, including Atlantis.

At first, the wondrous souls who came here from Mu for the "great adventure" had to adjust and acclimate to many new experiences. With the assistance and guidance of the angels, they were tutored inside the Royal Teton Retreat on how to live here, and gradually they ventured out and started to form small communities. As they adjusted and gained confidence, they ventured further and further away from the retreat. They later colonized the whole continent of Lemuria, which was huge and extended far into what you know today as the Pacific Ocean and beyond.

Before the fall, the Lemurians were not in physical expression as you know it today. Earth existed in a fifth dimensional expression at that time. Lemurians lived mainly in their fifth dimensional light bodies, with the ability to lower their vibration to experience denser levels whenever they chose and to return to their light bodies at will. Of course, this was very long ago, before what you call "the fall," which brought the gradual lowering in vibration of the consciousness of this wondrous race and of all others living on the planet. Our people, like many other civilizations, eventually fell to the level of the fourth dimension, and later on, all the way to the density of the third. This fall in consciousness took place over a period of several thousand years.

Opening to the Heart of Lemuria
Aurelia

A Bit of History of Lemuria's Tragic Ending

This information has been drawn from the teachings of Sharula Dux of Telos, now living on the "surface" in New Mexico, from several transmissions of various Ascended Masters during the Bridge to Freedom Dispensation in the 1950's, as well as other information channeled from Adama for this presentation.

The Lemurian Age stretched from approximately 4,500,000 BC to about 12,000 years ago. Until the sinking of the continents of Lemuria, and later of Atlantis, there were seven major continents on this planet. The lands belonging to the gigantic continent of Lemuria now under the Pacific Ocean include Hawaii, the Easter Islands, the Fiji Islands, Australia and New Zealand. The continent also encompassed lands in the Indian Ocean and Madagascar. The Eastern coast of Lemuria extended to California and part of British Columbia in Canada.

As a result of wars, great devastation took place on Lemuria and Atlantis. 25,000 years ago, Atlantis and Lemuria, the two highest civilizations of the time, battled each other over the direction of other civilizations on the planet. The Lemurians believed that less evolved cultures should be left alone to continue their evolution at their own pace, in accordance with their own understanding. The Atlanteans believed the less evolved cultures should be controlled by the two more evolved civilizations. This dissension caused a series of thermo-nuclear wars between them. When the wars were over and the dust had settled, there were no winners.

During these devastating wars, highly civilized people resorted to low levels of behavior, eventually realizing the futility of their actions. Ultimately, Atlantis and Lemuria became the victims of their own aggression, and the homelands of both continents were greatly weakened by war. The people, through the priesthood, were informed that within less than 15,000 years their continents would be destroyed. In these times, because people commonly lived an average of 20,000 to 30,000 years, it was understood that many who had caused the havoc would live to experience the destruction.

In the time of Lemuria, California was part of the Lemurian continent. When the Lemurians realized that their land was destined to perish, they petitioned Shamballa-the-Lesser, the head of the Agartha Network, for permission to build a city beneath Mount Shasta in order to preserve their culture and their records. Shamballa-the-Lesser is inhabited by the Hyperborean civilization which left the surface of this planet well over 40,000 years ago. The Hyperboreans were, at the time, in charge of making decisions for the Agartha Network. This network now consists of about 120 subterranean Cities of Light, mostly inhabited by Hyperboreans; four of the cities are Lemurian and a couple are Atlantean.

In order to be granted the permission to build a city and become part of the subterranean Agartha Network, the Lemurians had to prove to many agencies, such as the Galactic Confederation of Planets, that they had learned their lessons from the years of war and aggression. They also had to prove that they had learned the lessons of peace in order to be accepted again as members of the

Confederation. When permission was granted to build their city, it was understood that this area would survive the predicted cataclysms. There was already a very large dome cavern existing within Mount Shasta. The Lemurians constructed their city, Telos. This whole area, California, a major part of southwestern USA, the lands north of Mount Shasta along the west coast and up to British Columbia, was called Telos. Telos means communication with Spirit, oneness with Spirit and understanding with Spirit.

When Telos was constructed, it was designed for approximately 200,000 people. The continent was destroyed a bit earlier than anticipated and many people did not escape in time. When the cataclysm took place, only 25,000 people made it "inside" the mountain and were saved. Already, the records had been moved from Lemuria to Telos and several temples had been built.

It is known that the beloved Motherland went down overnight. The continent sank so quietly that most people were unaware of what was happening; most were asleep. No unusual weather conditions manifested that night. According to a transmission, given by Lord Himalaya in 1959 through Geraldine Innocenti *(El Morya's twin flame),* a great many of those in the priesthood who had remained faithful to the Light and their sacred calling kept their posts.

Another transmission from the Lord Maha Chohan *(March 1957 through Geraldine Innocenti, during the "Bridge to Freedom" dispensation)* stated, "Before the Lemurian continent sank, the priests and priestesses of the Temples were warned of the coming cataclysmic changes, and various focuses of the Sacred Fire were transported to Telos. Others were transported to other lands which would not be affected. Many of these Flames were taken to the continent of Atlantis to a specific location and were sustained there for quite a period of time by daily spiritual applications. Just before Lemuria sank, certain of these priests and priestesses returned to their homes on that continent and volunteered to go down with the land and Her people, giving the assistance of their radiation and extending comfort and fearlessness.

"They offered this help to counteract the fear which always comes with cataclysmic action. These loving benefactors, by the radiation of their sacrifice, literally surrounded the auras of the people in a blanket of peace and assisted in creating a freedom from fear so that the etheric bodies of those life-streams would not be so severely scarred; thus saving those people in future embodiments from having to experience greater tragic consequences."

Lord Himalaya in the "Bridge to Freedom" dispensation in 1959 said: "Many members of the priesthood placed themselves in small groups strategically in various areas and they prayed and sang as they went down beneath the water. The melody they sang was the same as is known today as '*Auld Lang Syne.*' The idea behind this action was that every horrifying experience leaves a very deep scar and trauma in the etheric body and cellular memory of the people, which takes several embodiments to heal.

"Through the action and the sacrifice of those of the priesthood, choosing to stay together in groups and singing to the very end, much fear was mitigated and a certain level of harmony was maintained. This way, the damage and trauma to the souls who perished was greatly diminished. It was said that those of the priesthood, along with the musicians, sang and prayed until the waves and the water had risen to the level of their mouths. It is then that they also perished. During the night, while the masses slept, under a starry blue sky, it was all over; the beloved Motherland was submerged beneath the waves of the Pacific Ocean. None of the priesthood had left their post and none had evidenced any fear. Lemuria went down with dignity!"

"Auld Lang Syne" was the last song ever heard in the land of Lemuria.

Tonight, I will ask you to sing this song again as part of our presentation. The people of Earth have brought this song forth again through the Irish people and very prophetic words have been added, "Should old acquaintances be forgot!" What do you think we are doing together this evening? Indeed, we are these old acquaintances reuniting again. Those of us from the third dimensional realm are now uniting in consciousness with our former friends and family members of Lemuria, "yet invisible" to our present sight. Hear this next statement well in your heart, my friends:

Before Lemuria sank completely, it was prophesied that one day, in some far distant future, many of us would gather in groups and sing this song again, with the absolute knowingness that the "Earth's Victory" is won.

Today brings the celebration of this long awaited day and the fulfilling of that incredible prophecy. Today, we are initiating the long awaited "Reunion." It is with tears in my eyes that I am letting you know from Adama that many of you in this room tonight were among those brave souls who sacrificed their lives for the benefit of the collective. Let's applaud your bravery then and rejoice now for our return to continue the great Lemurian mission of assisting humanity and the planet into her glorious ascension.

In Telos, one aspect of the mission has been to hold the balance and energies of ascension consciousness for the planet until such time that "surface" dwellers can do so for themselves. Now the time has come for our two civilizations to do this together as "One Heart."

17

Earth after the Sinking of the Two Continents

At the same time Lemuria was going down, Atlantis started shaking and loosing pieces of its continent. This continued for over 200 years until the final stage when it sank completely. For 2,000 years following the Lemurian and the Atlantean catastrophes, the planet continued to shake. Within 1,200 years the Earth lost two major land masses, a major setback and trauma which required several thousand years of recovery to restore balance. For hundreds of years after the destruction of both continents, so much debris was thrown into the atmosphere that the Earth did not experience bright daylight. The temperature dropped due to lack of sunlight and a large percentage of the animals and plants perished.

Why is there so little evidence today of the remains of these two great civilizations?

The cities that did not sink were reduced to rubble, or were wiped out by earthquakes or huge tidal waves that often flooded 1,000 miles inland, destroying most cities and habitation in their paths. Living conditions for the civilizations that survived those cataclysms was so harsh that people became frightened and the quality of life deteriorated quickly. For those who survived these calamities, hunger, poverty, and disease were their legacy.

The original height of mankind on this planet was approximately 12 feet. The Hyperboreans were and still are 12 feet tall; none of them live on the "surface" at this time. By the time Lemuria sank, Lemurians were reduced to 7 feet, and remain 7 to 8 feet tall to this day. Since then, there has been a further lowering of physical height on the planet. Most on the surface are 6 feet tall or less. As our civilization evolves, the greater body height will be restored. Even now, surface people are becoming taller than they were only 100 years ago.

This evening, if you choose to allow it, Adama and all those of Telos who are here in their light bodies are going to give us an opportunity to heal our own personal and planetary records. This will serve the planet and humanity, as well as each one of you individually.

The New Day, the New World, is just about to be born. We have learned our lessons of Love and the New Lemuria, the paradise refound, is just about to manifest again. Telos, the part of Lemuria that had remained faithful to Her sacred calling and the light, was lifted up to the fourth dimension at the time of the cataclysm. Her people eventually evolved into a fifth dimensional awareness, and exist in this higher dimension. Telos, our beloved Telos, with all the incredible people who live there, is our "Doorway" to this wondrous place.

Healing the Heart of Lemuria

Adama

Clearing of Lingering Old Lemurian Records At the Dawn of a New Era on Earth

My Beloveds, dearest brothers and sisters of the past, former family members,

On behalf of the Lemurian Council of Telos, on behalf of Ra and Rana Mu, king and queen of Telos, and also on behalf of about half a million of us present in our etheric bodies here this evening, it is with great joy, love and honoring that we greet you. As we open our hearts to you, we ask that you also open your hearts to us for a great healing.

We are here this evening to co-create together a very important clearing and healing for our planet and for all of you as well. Let's call this first a clearing of old, painful Lemurian records still lingering in the hearts and souls of most people. Secondly, by the reconnection of our hearts, let's create a new and more direct link between our two civilizations. The time of our separation is almost over and we are now reconnecting heart to heart with more and more of you everyday. This opening that we are just about to co-create, dear ones, will speed up the time of our emergence among you.

Soon, our two civilizations will meet once again, face to face in a great celebration of Light and Love. We will work together, hand in hand and heart to heart to build the most wondrous and magical permanent golden age of enlightenment, wisdom, peace and abundance you could ever imagine. We will assist you in building communities of Love and Light like never before without the interference from negative forces that have permeated this planet for so long.

The long dark night you have endured on the planet is almost over. Very soon, the light will shine brighter than it ever has for all of us to enjoy. You are now experiencing the last hours of darkness as the dawn is peeking through. Although you will soon be facing the changes that you have long anticipated, we ask you to perceive those changes as the "deliverance" of your planet. That time is now imminent and it is very important that you stay centered in your glorious Self. Do not allow yourself to go into fear, dear ones, and accept all changes and shifts that present themselves, no matter what you witness and experience around you. Embrace it all as the hand of God creating a new world for you.

So much help will be available to you from all directions, and we offer our assistance to you as well. Simply ask us in your heart and we will be there to assist you.

Aurelia Louise summarized the tragedy of the sinking of our continent 12,000 years ago. The purpose was to make you aware of the heavy records that were created by the devastation. We want you to know that many of those painful records still linger in the hearts and souls of humanity. The heartbreak and soul trauma that took place in those days is indescribable. It is now time to heal all of this, starting with your own being. These ancient records are causing a kind of spiritual fog in the consciousness of humanity. Because the pain has been so unbearable, too many of you have closed your consciousness to the remembrance of higher knowledge.

Myself, Adama, and all of us of Telos would like very much to clear a large percentage of those lingering records this evening. There are enough of us and you present that, if you set your intentions, we can create this healing for you and for the planet.

Would you like to accomplish this with us this evening? *(Yes, from the audience)*

Now, let us be silent for a few moments. I ask you to set your intention to have your own records cleared and healed. Go deep into your heart. Also present with us this evening are many masters and some from the angelic kingdom who are ready to assist with this major clearing. After you have asked for your own healing, ask silently in your heart for the same clearing and healing for all of humanity who are able at this time to be cleared. I assure you, there are many. *(Moment of silence)*

This, my friends, will start the ball rolling. It will roll, as in the hundredth monkey effect, until all records are cleared. It will assist humanity greatly. Thank you so much. By participating in this co-creation, you are rendering a major service to the planet and to yourself.

We took this energy you have just created around the planet to heal the hearts of many. Now that a large percentage of the records have been cleared and healed this evening, let us leave the tragedies and sorrows of the past behind and open up to the next great events that are now in the making, blessing our planet in ways you cannot yet comprehend. The doorway for us to connect heart to heart with humanity is now more open. We thank you for this planetary service and for your presence here this evening.

In a little while, be assured that the dark night will be completely lifted. There will be no more sorrows or tears on the surface of this planet. If there are tears, they will only be tears of joy and ecstasy. Together, we will manifest a most glorious destiny for all those who choose it.

We are your elder brothers and sisters who have volunteered to show you the way, to become your role models. Since we have already done what you are about to do, with our help, it will be much easier for you. We invite you to take our hands and accept our help. You know we have the ability to ease your journey in this next great planetary adventure. We have created the New Lemuria in the fifth dimension, a paradise of wonders and magic. All you ever dreamed about is here and much more. When the time comes, together with all of you, we will extend the New Lemuria to the "surface" of the planet. We will teach you all we know and all we have learned in the last 12,000 years of isolation from the surface population.

I am Adama, and along with my fellow Lemurians, we all champion your victory.

Chapter Three

The New Lemuria

Greetings, my friends, this is Adama.

There is a common belief among the surface population that Lemuria was destroyed under the waves of the Pacific Ocean over 12,000 years ago, and that it no longer exists. From a third dimensional perspective, this is entirely true. The cataclysm that destroyed most of our continent, along with almost 300 million of our people, created a painful devastation to the physical surface of the planet and its inhabitants.

It created a tremendous shock to Mother Earth. Almost overnight, in its final stage, our beloved Lemuria, considered the cradle of civilization for this planet, vanished. The rest of the world was utterly stunned, mourning the great loss. The pain of the loss of the Motherland was so great that, even today, most of you still carry pain and trauma deep in your cellular memory.

The souls who perished at the time were the most traumatized. Many of you who suffered the destruction of our continent have completely closed yourselves to the memory of your glorious Lemurian ancestry because, for you, the ending was so tragic. Your pain and grief has been buried deep within your subconscious, waiting for the time it can resurface and be healed. The purpose of this information is to assist you who read these words to begin consciously healing those records, within yourselves and the planet. For this, my dear brothers and sisters, with great love and compassion, we offer you our assistance.

Lemuria still exists to this day in a fifth dimensional frequency, not yet visible to your third dimensional vision and perception.

To all of you still feeling the grief of the loss, let us share with you that Lemuria has never been totally destroyed, as perceived in your present understanding. As the veil between dimensions continues to thin, we want to assure you that in a not too distant future, for those engaged in the ascension process, your beloved Lemuria, in Her new Splendor and Glory, will reveal Herself to you in a very physical and tangible manner.

As you open yourselves up to a more conscious way of living, and release distorted and erroneous belief systems you have embraced in the last millennia, you will be able to perceive the beloved Motherland again. Eventually you will be allowed to step in to be received by Her with all the Love and Magnificence She now has to offer. When you are ready, you will be invited to join us consciously in this place of paradise. At the time of the blast, Lemuria and what it represented to the planet was lifted into a fourth dimensional frequency which later evolved into the fifth. It continued to thrive and evolve to the level of perfection and beauty it has now reached, inhabited by those who were saved when Lemuria sank.

If this information brings tears to your eyes, open your heart to heal the pains that have been buried within you for so very long. Let your grief flow! Allow your tears to bring healing to every part of your being. Allow yourself to really feel it and embrace it in your heart through the breath. Allow all remembrances and pain to be felt fully without suppressing anything. This is how you will bring forth your healing, increment by increment. As you inhale the pain through the breath, those imprints will dissolve and be healed forever. Ask your Higher Self to assist you in uncovering those records that are keeping you from moving forward towards your new glorious reality.

In your daily meditation, we ask you to do this work faithfully until you feel completion. Connect with us and with our Love, heart to heart. Ask for our assistance and we will be there with you as you do this most important inner work. All of us in Telos are eager to assist all of you who will reach out to us in your hearts. We are a civilization which has achieved great heart openings and our vibration pulses with the Heart of the Divine Mother. Gradually, the deep-seated pain will be lifted and you will feel much lighter. The clearing of this pain will also assist you in the opening of your remembrance and the perceiving of your true identity. It will allow you to make giant leaps into your full spiritual, emotional and physical evolution and renewal.

We invite you to come to Telos at night while your body sleeps. We have many spiritual counselors who are willing to work with you. Each one who comes is assigned three counselors who will work with you very closely. One focuses on healing the emotional body, another focuses on healing the mental body and the third focuses on healing the etheric body, all together in oneness with your Divine Presence.

Our channel, Aurelia Louise, was granted some time ago, the opportunity for a momentary glimpse into the New Lemuria. She was deeply touched, and knows with absolute certainty in her heart that what we are communicating through her is not a promise that remains in the distant future. She knows with every cell of her being that this manifestation could become a reality within this decade for many of you. The journey is yours to step into! Will you take our hands and ride the wave of ascension with us into a new dimensional reality?

As Earth Beings, We Are One Big Family

From where we reside, we observe consistent progress in the great awakening taking place within the consciousness of human beings as they remember their divine nature.

Dear ones, as much as you may not yet see the full picture of this wondrous advancement, we have the technology to see this progress and make graphs of it on our amino acid computers. We can chart the raising of vibrational frequency by mankind day by day in any area on the surface. Each day, we notice more people awakening to their divine purpose and making a new choice to embrace love and peace within their heart, in their personal lives and for the planet.

The very fact that there are so many of you now awakening to a greater understanding of true spirituality, and making new choices for yourselves, shows us that your eventual victory and spiritual freedom are assured. It is only a question of how long and how many Earth years it will take to reach critical mass. We can honestly tell you that it is happening even faster than originally expected by the spiritual hierarchy. In any case, you are no longer looking at centuries or millennia for the transition into the new world that you have been anticipating for so long. Know that within ten years, many positive changes will have already taken place, and from then on, you will live through an intense accelerated cycle of positive changes. The intensity of the energy will not stop or diminish until you are comfortably nestled in the wonders and the bliss of the fifth dimension.

The time of reunion for our two
civilizations is finally very close.

In Telos, along with your brothers and sisters of the "Earth Within," a vast empire of many civilizations, we are watching this expansion of consciousness with great joy and anticipation. We always support you with our Love and our Light. We are like children counting the number of days before Christmas, the "Christmas" of our "Uniting" in Love and Brotherhood as one big Earth family. We watch with wonder the awakening taking place day by day, and we know that the time for reunion of our two civilizations is finally very close, after so many centuries of physical separation.

When the time of our emergence to the surface dimension comes, it will be a time of love and great rejoicing for many, particularly for those who are consciously aware of our presence within the Earth, and who experience a deep yearning to finally greet and talk with us face-to-face. The wonders of our "Great Encounter" will be even greater than you can imagine at this time. Be assured that we long to be with you in a more tangible way just as much as you long to be with us. We are family sharing a mutual desire.

We are also watching a great number of light-workers who have embodied at this time to assist with this wondrous mission, leading the way in this grand awakening. You are brave warriors of Light, facing many difficulties to assist the Christing of the planet, and we hold you so preciously in our hearts. It is with gratitude and profound love that we salute and honor you.

We will return to the "surface" in a more tangible way when the spiritual awakening has reached critical mass, not sooner. Shortly, we will be granted permission to start mixing with a limited number of "surface" people who have attained the level of frequency that allows them to see us and be comfortable in the presence of our level of radiance. Be sure that we will not lower our vibration to meet you in your present level of third dimensional density. However, we will most likely meet you over halfway. In order for any of you to perceive us in the high levels of the fourth dimension, you will have already raised your own frequency and consciousness to that level.

This primary exchange will gradually open the pathways for our eventual greater emergence among you, joining both civilizations as One Big Family of the Children of the Mother. We are beings of love, we live a path of love and we want you to know that we have much love for all of you.

When we come, we will be able to teach you a way of life that will help you establish the foundations for a permanent golden age of enlightenment, love, peace, beauty and prosperity for all.

We will assist you in ushering in this long anticipated golden age. Prepare by loving each other more and by seeing each other more like brothers and sisters of a huge family. In your mind and heart, begin to be receptive to us and invite us to become your guides and mentors. You shall never regret it.

For the last 12,000 years that we have been living "underground," we have established a foundation based on the consciousness of love and true Brotherhood in the multi-dimensional cities and in Telos. Over these thousands of years, we have refined the structures of our societies to attain greater and greater levels of resonance with Divine Principles in every aspect of our lives.

Beloved ones, we have witnessed your pain and struggle long enough. It is with much gladness and expectation that we are waiting to show you the way of manifesting this higher-dimensional reality in your world, so that never again will there be suffering on this planet for humanity or any of the other kingdoms evolving here.

It will not take 12,000 years to accomplish
this with our help. We already know how.

The melding of our energies through the magic of "Love"
can and will bring these wonderful changes for you. Be willing to open your hearts to us and trust that we are not only
your friends, but also your brothers and sisters of long ago.
At a soul level, we all know each other very well, as we were
all family at one time on the great continent of Lemuria.
And we still are.

We send you much love from Telos. We generate it with ease
which allows us to live in great opulence. We hold you dearly
in our hearts. Until we meet, keep practicing the art of true
love, which starts with loving yourself. May love abound
in your heart for self, for each other and for all of creation.
You are precious jewels and expressions of the Love of the
Father/Mother God!

Part Two

Messages from Adama,
High Priest of Telos

The attitude of gratitude
Opens the doors to miracles,
And the multiplication of your blessings!
If you feel a lack of blessings in your life
Or desire to expand your blessings
To a greater level,
Practice this ancient art,
To improve all areas of your life,
Including your abundance.
- Adama

Chapter Four

Government of Telos

Adama has channeled some of this information, while another portion comes from the writings of Sharula Dux, a member of the Telosian community, now living on the surface.

In Telos, there are two forms of government. The king and queen of Telos, Ra and Rana Mu, are ascended masters who are also twin flames. They are the ultimate rulers of Telos, forming one aspect of its government.

The second form of government is the local Council, called the Lemurian Council of Light of Telos. It consists of 12 ascended masters, with 6 men and 6 women serving on the council to balance the divine masculine with the divine feminine. A thirteenth member, the head High Priest of Telos, who at this time is Adama, officiates as the leader of the council. He makes the final determination when there is a tied vote in the decisions made by the council.

Members of the council are selected according to their level of spiritual attainment, inner qualities, maturity and area of expertise. When a member of the council decides to move on to another level of service, the vacancy is made known to our people. Those who desire to take a seat on the council may apply. All applications are carefully studied by the council, by the members of the priesthood, and by the king

33

and queen of Telos. The king and the queen have the final word in choosing a council member.

The City of Telos

Telos is a fairly large community, with approximately one and one half million people. We are divided into several villages, and we all share the local government. What we call the city of Telos is divided into five levels of several square miles each.

The first level
The largest percentage of our people live beneath the dome on the first level. This is also where the administrative and public buildings and several temples are located. In the center of this level stands our main temple, called the temple of Ma-Ra, a pyramid shaped structure. It will seat 10,000 people. This temple is dedicated to the priesthood of Melchizedek. The pyramid is white, with the capstone, called the "living stone," donated to us by Venus.

The second level
This is where all the production and manufacturing for the people and the city takes place. Several schools, for children and adults, are located here and many of our people live on this level as well.

The third level
This level is dedicated to our hydroponic gardens. All of our food is grown on about seven acres of land, producing a diet that is interesting, fun, and offers great variety. Our methods of gardening are so effective that seven acres of land is all that is needed. We grow a very large variety of food and feed one and one half million people, creating strong, healthy bodies that do not age.

I want you to be aware that we eat, yes, but as fifth dimensional beings, we do not have to eat like you do. We eat only if and when we want to and can manifest at will what we want. Our food is not as dense as yours. Though it has substance, taste, color and form, to your third dimension perception, it would be considered etheric food.

Our hydroponic gardens are able to produce crops on a constant basis. We can grow food much faster, using advanced hydroponic technology. We use very little soil, much water, and no chemicals. Our food is totally organic and carries the highest vibration. Our form of gardening does not need fertilizers and does not deplete the soil. We do add organic minerals to the water for the plants. Our crops are also enhanced and quickened by the great light, energy and love vibration of Telos. This is the magic of our fifth dimensional consciousness that you will soon discover, possibly in this decade or early in the next.

The fourth level
This level contains some hydroponic gardening, some manufacturing, and a large area for nature in a park-like setting with small lakes and fountains.

The fifth level
This area is devoted to nature. There are tall trees and lakes in a park-like atmosphere. This is where we keep all our animals. On this level, many plants and animals have been preserved that you no longer have on the surface. Our animals are vegetarians and do not eat each other. They live side by side in total harmony, without fear or aggression toward people or each other. Telos is really the place where the lion and the lamb lie side-by-side and sleep together in total confidence.

Transportation in Telos

We have several modes of transportation within the city, such as moving sidewalks, inter-level elevators and electromagnetic sleds resembling snowmobiles. For travel between cities, residents take *"the Tube,"* an electromagnetic subway system capable of speeds up to 3,000 m.p.h.

Physical Appearance of the Telosians

Is your physical appearance very different from ours?

Essentially we look the same, although we are taller and broader in stature. We have maintained a youthful look for thousands of years, appearing between 20 to 40 years of age, as chosen. In our society, no one shows signs of aging nor do we grow gray hair with the passing of time. This may appear strange to you at first, but you will get used to it rather quickly. We can change our look quite easily at will. The gift of living in perfected bodies comes with the grace of ascension into a fifth dimensional consciousness.

When you are introduced to someone 20,000 years of age, you will notice that he or she looks as youthful as anyone else. Since we have reached the state of immortality, we prolong our life in our present body as long as we choose. When we feel it is time to move on to another service or a higher dimension, we take our bodies with us into our new evolutionary adventure.

Celebration of Holidays

Do you have Holidays in Telos,
and how do you celebrate them?

I greet you with beautiful flowers from my heart. Yes, we have wonderful holidays in Telos, with grand and elaborate festivities in which everyone participates, including the children. Although we do not generally celebrate the same holidays you do, we perceive our lives each day as a continu-

36

ous celebration of life, of love and of deep gratitude in our hearts for the beauty, the bounty and the grace we enjoy every day.

Although we have many reasons to celebrate, our main festivities take place four times a year with the change of seasons during the solstices and equinoxes. During that time every city of the Agartha network initiates sophisticated three-day celebrations. These great celebrations are organized all over the cities, and friends and families participate together and display much love for one another. A great number of people travel to various cities to join the festivities and visit with those they love. In Telos during these times, our population almost doubles with visitors from all over the Earth's interior, and many who come from the stars. These visitors are members of our galactic family and your family also. In the near future, many of you will meet consciously and tangibly with many of your brothers and sisters from the stars. This will bring you so much joy!

We all join in communion for a grand celebration of love and oneness with our Creator, with the Earth and with each other. We dance, we play music, we sing and we display our love and appreciation for the joy we experience together. Prior to each celebration, we all contribute to the decoration of our city, which we do with exquisite creativity and beauty. No effort is spared, and through the decorations alone, one enters into the celebrations.

Throughout the year, we have several other occasions for which we set aside time for celebration. If we do not have specific reasons to celebrate, we create some. Life is so magical and full of surprises that there is always a reason to celebrate. We also celebrate your love and your openings to your ancient Lemurian heritage. In our hearts, we are preparing the grand celebrations for the reunion of the two civilizations, which will indeed create the greatest of all celebrations.

37

We Live in Circular Homes

We hear that the Lemurians live in "circular homes." Can you describe them?

At one time we had to build our homes the way you do now with the assistance of architects, real physical plans and various building materials and tools such as saws and hammers. Now that we have become fifth dimensional beings, we create our homes by manifesting much of what we need with our thoughts, intentions and sustained focus.

Yes, we design our homes on the principles of sacred geometry. For this reason, most of our homes are circular in one way or another, and are designed with great creativity and beauty. The basic material for the exterior of our homes is crystal. Always keep in mind that I speak from a fifth dimensional perspective. You must do your best to understand my words from the viewpoint of that perspective. What we as masters attempt to describe to you does not have an exact counterpart in your dimension. Some of these descriptions may not make sense to you if you view them only from a third dimensional perspective.

Everything we have and create, including our bodies, look and feel very physical to us. In fact, our physicality feels as real to us as your physicality feels to you. Our physicality is imbued with so much light that it has lost most of its density, and would not be visible or tangible to you in your present state of consciousness.

The reality of our dimension is very fluid, and nearly all of us can create all we want and need almost instantly. We have now attained the ability to create our homes very quickly, any way we desire, and we can make changes almost as rapidly any time we want. It will take you a little while on the surface to fully understand this and to be able to do the same. It will soon become great fun for you to learn the practical application of these concepts in greater depth and begin to experiment with them, at first under our supervision and with our assistance. When you are ready, this is one of the many things we are longing to teach you.

Our homes are constructed from crystal-like stones that emit much light and are quite beautiful. The stones contain enough opacity to prevent those on the outside from looking in. In this way we maintain our privacy at all times. When we are inside, however, the view looking out is totally clear, like houses of clear glass allowing us to see out at all angles and in all directions. This is why we feel that we live in crystal palaces. Our view of the outside is never obstructed by anything and we never feel enclosed by walls.

I would like to explain in simple terms how we would begin to create a small circular home. For the fun of it, I want to give you an idea of how we proceed. For the completion of the home, we use the same principles. You can use your imagination to finish this home for yourself, as you wish, and start dreaming your very own home. It is all about consciously creating your dreams and manifesting them.

Now let me proceed with the creation of a small circular home.

First - I decide on the location and how large in diameter I desire this home to be.

Second - With my mind and intention I begin visualizing in detail the outline of the structure I want to create. If I am not specific enough, or if I become sloppy with my visualization, the structure will not manifest the way I intend. Remember, I use my mind and heart energy to create what I want. The material I use in my mind is a crystal-like substance. In my mind, I begin to visualize laying each stone in the right order and place, and with the exact design I want the finished product to manifest. At this point, it is still just

Telos

an outline, not yet filled in or densified. Believe me, I can do this quite rapidly. Since we live in a no-time zone, it really does not matter how long it takes. In your time it would not take me more than a half hour.

Third - When I am completely satisfied with the creation of the outline of my new crystalline structure and I feel my heart bursting with joy over this new creation, I proceed to the next step. It is now time to fill each stone with a greater intensity of crystalline light and bring more density into it. As I continue to focus intently on my new creation, the outline of each stone fills with the light and love I pour into it. When this is complete, I continue my focus on densifying the light from which the stones are created until they reach the desired opacity.

And so it is, my dear friends, the crystalline structure of the new home is now completed. It is ready to be finished any way you want with all the beauty you choose to add to it. When you hold enough light and love in your consciousness, all types of manifestations become easy and completely natural. Go now about your daily business in Love and Gratitude for all that you have, and create anew with much beauty the type of life you have been longing for. You can all do it when you believe that you can.

Please take note ...

Please take note that what we explain here exists in a fifth dimensional vibration. It is not as physical as yours, nor does it possess the kind of physical density you are accustomed to in the third dimension. If you were to come here in your present state, most of you on the surface would not be able to perceive anything at our level of physicality. Our physicality feels as real to us as yours does to you. It represents a level of physicality, however, that is so full of light that we no longer experience limitations of any kind. Our dimension is not visible or perceivable to your present state of awareness and spiritual awakening. Do not let this discourage you; it will all evolve. As you open your hearts wider and progress on your journey towards divine union, all will open to your awareness. You will embrace and manifest more and more of your divinity in your present physical incarnation. Continue to trust that the veils will soon begin to lift for all those who yearn for the ultimate union, and do the spiritual work needed to reach that level of evolution.

Tunnels Inside the Earth

How are the tunnels between the underground cities and those from the Inner Earth maintained?

The tunnels between the "subterranean" cities, the Middle Earth and the Inner Earth require little maintenance, if any. They have been constructed to be maintenance free. From time to time, when there is a serious earthquake or a volcanic eruption somewhere on the surface of the planet, some of the tunnels may be slightly damaged. However, with our advanced technology, we get together and fix the problems very quickly. The tunnels are very rarely damaged. The advanced technology we use is shared by all civilizations inside the Earth.

Do their officials meet on a regular basis?

Yes, we often have council meetings with officials of various civilizations inside the Earth. We are all very friendly and loving with each other. There are never any power struggles among us. Unconditional love is always the master rule. Our main reason for meeting is to discuss how we can best find ways of collaborating with each other in the most efficient manner for the benefit of all. We discuss trade with each other. We have no monetary system, and share any surplus of goods and food among ourselves. We also discuss ways of assisting "surface" folks with their evolution and spiritual initiations.

Shamballa and Her Role

What is the role of Shamballa, its origin, its government and main purpose, today and in the future?

The city of Shamballa is no longer a physical city. It has not been for a very long time. It now holds a fifth, sixth and seventh dimensional vibration. It still exists on the etheric level. It is basically the etheric headquarters for this planet, the home of Sanat Kumara and those assisting him. Although Sanat Kumara has now officially returned to Venus, he maintains a focus in Shamballa and is still assisting our planet. Mount Shasta, the Royal Teton Retreat in Wyoming and Shamballa are the main locations where the spiritual hierarchy of the planet live, meet and hold their conclaves. Shamballa and these other places hold a permanent focus of spiritual government for the planet. Of course, there are several other important etheric focuses throughout the planet.

Inhabitants of the Earth's Interior

In the Middle and Inner Earth reside many very ancient civilizations which eons ago came from other worlds and universes. They are all in an ascended state of consciousness, although several have retained some level of physicality. They live mostly in a fifth and sixth dimensional awareness and higher.

The Agartha Network consists of about 120 "subterranean" Cities of Light, mostly inhabited by Hyperboreans. At least four of the cities are inhabited by Lemurians, and a few are inhabited by Atlanteans. The beings living in the subterranean cities close to the surface vibration are also in the ascended state, but have retained a certain level of physicality. Shamballa-the-Lesser had been the governing city of the Agartha Network. It is inhabited by the Hyperboreans. The city of Telos is now the governing city of the Agartha Network.

Other Cities of the Agartha Network

POSID: Primary Atlantean outpost, located beneath the Mato Grosso plains region of Brazil. Population: 1.3 million.

SHONSHE: Refuge of the Uighur culture, a branch of the Lemurians who chose to form their own colonies 50,000 years ago. The entrance is guarded by a Himalayan lamasery. Population: 3/4 million.

RAMA: Remnant of the surface city of Rama, India located near Jaipur. Inhabitants are known for their classic Hindu features. Population: 1 million.

SHINGWA: Remnant of the northern migration of the Uighurs. Located on the border of Mongolia and China, with a small secondary city in Mount Lassen, California.

What is the quality
Of the internal dialogue
That you entertain within yourself
Moment by moment?
Does it reflect what you desire to attain?
- Adama

Chapter Five

Emergence Update

Many of you already know that a great number of us are planning to eventually emerge to the surface when enough of you are ready and willing to receive us along with our teachings. It will be our pleasure to reconnect with all of you face-to-face and teach you all we know.

We will teach you how to create a life of magic for yourself and your loved ones, right where you are. We ask you to assist in spreading the awareness of our presence within Mount Shasta to all those whose consciousness is ready to receive this information. Do what you can to support our emergence to the "surface," and it is my promise that you will never regret it.

We notice that many of you want to know time and dates; some of you are impatient. We ask you to understand that the time of our emergence does not depend on us; we are ready. It is the surface population, the collective, which is not yet ready to receive us. To come out prematurely would defeat the purpose of our emergence and create definite setbacks.

What will be required of us for you to come out?

First of all, we monitor and register the love and light

quotient of the surface population. We measure the level of compassion and heart opening of the collective. At this time, it is about 65%. For us to join you will require a percentage of about 90%. This is only one of the factors we examine. There are several others we also consider very important. Much will depend on the level of consciousness and evolution of the collective, awareness of the higher vibrations of love, and willingness to live life as divine beings.

You are now embarked on the grand adventure of ascension. Those who will be able to stay on the planet beyond the next decade are those who have chosen to embrace their Christhood and Divinity. Personal and planetary events are going to become your mentors to assist you in that direction. After millions of years of evolution on this planet, our Earth Mother has chosen to move on in Her own personal evolution and to take along with Her those of humanity who are ready to make the same choice.

As a result of her choice, the Creator has given the Earth a mighty dispensation of Light and Love. Your planet is now flooded with new energies unlike any before. These energies are increasing in intensity, velocity and frequency with each passing day. Seven major gateways have opened from the Creator Source in 2002 that will greatly transform your planet by the year 2012 and beyond. In a hundred years from now, your planet will be totally transformed.

Each of those gateways contains a number of sub-gateways and portals that all of you must pass through in order to move on to the next step. By 2012, or perhaps a bit sooner, many of the "initiates" will be lifted to a fifth dimensional reality, into a world of magic and paradise. In a short while, your planet will be transformed enough to be almost unrecognizable compared to your present standards of living.

The intensity of Light is increasing daily. This will assist you in the great transformation that is needed for your passage into the greatest adventure of all of your lifetimes. The bottom line is "you will have to embrace your Christhood or get off the planet." For this you will be given more assistance than ever before.

This is the meaning of the second coming. All life on Earth will soon return to the original perfection it was endowed with at the beginning of Her creation. There are other planets like Earth where people are still enjoying separation from God and the way of violence. There will be many new choices for the souls who decide to stay behind.

What does this have to do with our emergence? Beloved brothers and sisters, we are looking forward to joining with you as much as you are with us. We will not come to the surface until the majority of the people on this planet have embraced love, compassion and harmlessness toward all life forms and all kingdoms. It will also be necessary for a certain percentage of the population, not yet determined, to be aware of us and welcome our emergence. These two factors will determine the time of our emergence, and as well as several other considerations.

We hope that by 2006 or 2007 or shortly thereafter, enough positive changes in the heart of humanity and in the political scene will have occurred to allow us to emerge in greater numbers. We wish to assist you, along with your Earth Mother, in going the rest of the way in your ascension process.

When you ask us for the dates of our emergence, we turn the question back to you by asking if you have yet met the requirements. Dear ones, when will you and the collective be ready to receive us? It is really up to you to do your homework and prepare yourself and others who are open for the awesome experience of our emergence among you.

Do you have an emergence plan?

Yes, we do. We have an emergence plan that must remain undisclosed, one that will unfold in a clandestine way. At first, in various places, we will meet secretly with small groups of people to give them direct teachings and transmissions of our love and energies. These small groups will then go out and transmit our teachings to others who are ready and willing to hear. As more people become ready to meet with us, the circle will expand and gradually grow into large groups.

As this momentum grows, more of us will come out to assist. When enough of these groups are formed around the planet, and their members have kept their covenant with us, we will then gradually allow more and more people to meet directly with us, until we have fully emerged among you.

It might also please you to know that several of our people are already doing wondrous work in your dimension to prepare the way. None of them are allowed yet to identify themselves to "surface" folks. They are here incognito, and this is the way it must remain for the time being. Unless your vibration, alignment and motivation resonate with a fifth dimensional consciousness, they will not contact you.

The second wave of our greater emergence will not take place in the third dimensional frequency.

The rest of us will not lower our vibration to your level. Understand that we may be physical, but we vibrate at a frequency that is much higher and faster than yours, and thus we are invisible to most of you as yet. It is your job to raise your vibration and consciousness at least two-thirds of the way to meet ours. This means that you will have to elevate your vibration almost to a fifth dimensional level in order to meet us consciously.

This means that as a greater number of us mingle casually among you, initially there will be those who will see us just as tangibly as you see each other. There will, however, be a majority who do not. Gradually, it will come to pass that more and more "surface" folks will raise their vibration and will join the ranks of those who can see and interact with us.

We will then have an engagement together, if you choose to meet the conditions. With open hearts, we are awaiting your readiness. We bless you and hold each one of you very dear in our souls.

I am Adama.

Perfection is a state of beingness
That keeps expanding forever
Unto eternity.
No matter how perfect
Any state of being one reaches,
There is always a greater level
To open and expand into.
This is what creates the magic
Of enlightenment.
- Ahnahmar

Chapter Six

Telos Codes of Entry

From those of you who have become aware of our existence beneath Mount Shasta, we feel a great longing to visit Telos and meet us face to face. We feel your great desire to experience the wonders and magic of an enlightened civilization, and to reconnect with your former family members who are living in Telos or elsewhere in the fifth dimension.

On the inner plane, we feel your longing and hear your thoughts. "When can we come to visit Telos?" "When will the doors of Telos be opened to surface dwellers?" Beloved ones, we want to share with you that your long wait will soon come to an end. We foresee that it could very well happen before the end of this decade. We will begin to invite small groups from the surface for a visit. We would like you to experience what can be accomplished in your world when the majority of the population adopts our way of life. You will acquire a totally new perspective on how wonderful life on this planet can be if lived according to divine principles and true brotherhood.

It is important for you to realize that at first, and for quite some time, the visitations will be made by personal invitation only. Do not be concerned with how these invitations are expressed. When your turn to be invited comes, we have many ways of communicating with you, no matter where you live. Because we live in a fifth dimensional awareness, we exercise a strict code of entry for all those who are invited. Be assured that your personal invitation will not be forthcoming until you meet the requirements of that code of entry.

To explain in detail the full implication of our requirements is not the purpose of this message. Nevertheless, let me give you a general overview of what will be required.

First of all, only those who have attained close to a fifth dimensional awareness in their consciousness will qualify. This means that they will have embraced unconditional love for Self and for others, as well as for all parts of life and all kingdoms. Duality consciousness needs to be released by at least 90%. It is also important to have balanced your masculine and feminine energies and cultivated harmlessness in every area of your life. I leave it to you to search your heart for what this all means. This is your homework, dear ones. It will lead you to Self-discovery, to the wonders of who you really are and the qualities of Divine Self that have eluded you for so long.

Second, you need to clear and heal your emotional and mental bodies of all negativity, past and present. All past and present records of pain, anger, grief, guilt, sorrow, trauma, shame, addiction, hopelessness, low self-esteem, negative imprints, miasms, etc., must be embraced and released from your subconscious mind, solar plexus and emotional body. Because of the high energy vibration of Telos, any emotions or thought-forms of a vibration less than divine love would be amplified over a thousandfold in your mind and feelings. Unless these records have been cleared, it would not be possible for you to stay in our vibration for more than a few minutes without experiencing trauma.

Third, only those who have completed their seventh spiritual initiation and have attained or nearly attained readiness for the ceremonies of their ascension will fulfill our codes of entry. On this planet, the Office of the Christ under Lord Maitreya and Lord Sananda *(known as your beloved Jesus in his Earth ministry 2000 years ago)* is the place where you can apply to receive these initiations on the inner planes.

Most of you are not consciously aware that these initiations take place on the inner planes. However, they do take place and are governed by how you consciously live your daily life. Passing these initiations and moving on to ascension and spiritual freedom has been the goal of your many incarnations on this planet. The seventh initiation is certainly not the end of your evolution, but our codes of entry require that a candidate must reach this level of initiation to enter Telos. With the new dispensations now available, these initiations can be completed much faster than ever before in the history of Earth's evolution. What used to take thousands of years to achieve can now be accomplished, if you choose, within the next 10 to 20 years.

For each requirement just mentioned, there are many ramifications. It is not our desire to make you feel that these goals are unattainable or to inspire hopelessness. We know that it is possible for many of you to attain this level of consciousness in a reasonable amount of time. Several thousand people on the planet have already reached these levels of initiation and beyond in the last few years. You may find them among the people you meet in daily life, although they are not necessarily identifiable. Those who have attained this level and know it, usually keep this information to themselves. Many more are constantly being added to the ranks of those who have achieved this level.

We mention these requirements because many of you are familiar with us but are not aware of Telos' codes of entry. Everyone who enters our doors, no matter who they are or where they come from, must attain the level of spiritual development needed to be introduced to a fifth dimensional vibration.

As you diligently do your spiritual work and gain momentum on your pathway of ascension, you will soon achieve these goals. Open your heart to love, and you will find that the initiations are much easier to pass through than continuing to experience the difficulty in which you find yourselves. The refinement that these initiations bring to your consciousness will open the doors not only to Telos, but also to the New Lemuria and other places of magic and wonder.

Remember always that Love is the key, dear ones. Love will open all doors to you and quickly propel you on your pathway to limitless spiritual freedom. From Love you came and to Love you now return.

I am Adama, your Lemurian brother.

Chapter Seven

The Children of Telos

Do some of your children have direct contact with other children living on the surface?

No. Our children have not had any contact with surface folks for several hundred years. We hope and foresee that this will change towards the end of this decade. The only contact our children have with surface people is through your television. Yes, we access your television network in Telos and we screen certain programs for the enjoyment of our children.

Do children from other inner cities meet each other?

They certainly do. We share holidays and celebrations, often visiting in various subterranean cities and bringing our children along. We are a very open culture and we like to socialize and dance. We often visit friends and families from other cultures or cities, and they come to visit us. The doors are always open. There is no need for a special occasion for those visits. We all travel quite regularly between the various cities of the Agartha Network and other inner cities. When parents make those trips for whatever reason—social, familial or business—the children are usually invited to come along if they wish. Since it is always a treat for them, they rarely decline.

The Future of Our Children

What does the future hold between your children and ours?

When our two civilizations merge together as one, our children will also merge with your children. Your children and our children are basically not so different. The merging of our children with yours will be carefully planned. It will be a lot of fun and a great adventure for the children of both civilizations.

It has been said many times that this planet is rapidly moving forward with the necessary shifts that will allow Her to host exclusively an enlightened civilization. This means, my friends, that in a not-so-far-distant future the Dark Age on this planet will fade away. Our two civilizations will unite as one, including the children, for the glorious ascension we have been awaiting for so long.

Let's all embrace and welcome the dawning new world. As the Phoenix rises out of the ashes, a brand new world of divine love and perfection will rise up with the crumbling of all your old limiting belief systems. You will let go of outmoded governmental systems of control and manipulation that you have been programmed with for eons of time.

Compare the Earth to the Phoenix. She will rise and take you along with Her. But first, you must let go of all that no longer serves you. You must be willing to let go of the old "outmoded" ways of life that have kept you in limitation and pain for so long. The ashes represent the purification that the Earth and all humanity will first go through. Your future is bright, my friends. Keep your hopes alive for yourselves and your children. A most wondrous world is awaiting them and this is why they are here. They will show you the way; in their souls they already know how!

Growing Up in Telos

This section is partly channeled information from Adama through Aurelia Louise Jones as well as information published by Sharula Dux of Telos in 1996.

In Telos, only when a couple is united in a sacred marriage are they allowed to have children. Since parenting in Telos is a long-term project, couples desiring to have children must first take special parenting training. On the surface you must go through driver's education and have a license to drive a car, but any inexperienced, emotionally unstable sixteen year old child can give birth. These surface children participate in this all important responsibility of bringing another life into the world without any preparation or understanding of life itself.

Children born in Telos spend a full two years in twenty-four-hour care with both mother and father. This is most crucial to the psychological make-up of the child. The father takes the first two years of the child's life off from his civil duties so that the infant can have balanced and equal time with the earthly representatives of Father/Mother God. Since the government provides all necessities for living, the two-year period is ensured for the parents.

A newborn child in Telos will receive a set of ten godparents soon after birth. This has many advantages. In Telos, a child will never feel that he/she does not receive enough attention with an additional twenty doting parental figures to guide them through their early years. It is usually arranged that all ten sets of godparents chosen will have newborn children of their own. This way, even if you are an only child, you will always have surrogate brothers and sisters to interact and play with. As the child grows, it will spend time living with each set of godparents. This instills a subconscious acceptance that Father/Mother God will always

57

be present since so much love from varying sources is available. Children learn early on that they will always be loved and provided for.

Children begin schooling at the age of three and their basic education continues until they reach the age of eighteen. Between three and five years, five days a week, they attend a half-day of organized play directed at learning basic social and art skills. Basics such as colors and numbers are taught in fun games. From five years on, they are in school for a full day, just like schools in your civilization.

The language taught in school is, of course, Lemurian as Telos is a Lemurian culture. The Lemurian language originates from the universal language of our galaxy, known as Solara Maru. Other planetary root languages like Sanskrit, Hebrew and Egyptian also trace their origins back to Solara Maru. While the English language is not mandatory for students, it is taught as an optional second language. Naturally, it is much desired that our people learn English and nearly everyone does, since Telos is located in an English-speaking country and the radio and television shows from the surface are monitored for our enjoyment!

All the children's desks are equipped with computers that link them to the Universal Energy and Information Grid. Since our computer network runs on amino acids, a living force, it taps into the akashic records and higher elements of the Christ Directive and cannot be corrupted. Consequently, it provides historical information that is accurate and truthful.

The teachers in all the schools in Telos are trained Melchizedek priests and priestesses. When Telosian youngsters are old enough to get into some serious mischief, about the age of twelve, and need more time with others their own age, they enter what is termed the "Group." This group is a sorority/fraternity of children their own age.

These groups of ten to twenty will experience all the wonders of puberty and adolescence together. Made up equally of girls and boys, the "group" forms a bond that carries them into adulthood and beyond. A Melchizedek priest and priestess from the Temple will be selected to guide the group through various stages of growth. The group format is also used in their schooling process and all learning is experienced together.

Group members will experience, share, experiment with, discuss and grow through the various issues of adolescence. The "group" is especially effective in handling the classic teenage problem of resentment. This issue activates everyone into finding a creative outlet for the problem. Group members usually become close, lifelong friends, encountering and sharing all of life's milestones together.

At the age of eighteen and the completion of basic education, an individual then chooses the direction he/she wants to take for the next few years of their life. One option always available to them is advanced studies in the field of their choosing. Vast collections of records from advanced civilizations of the past are stored in record-keeper crystals in the libraries of Telos. Occasionally, though not often, a teen will choose to go directly into the Melchizedek Temple and begin spiritual training as a temple neophyte.

Another option is to go straight into service in the Silver Fleet *(Fleet of Telosian spaceships)*. Since all subterranean cities are active members of the Confederation, it is everyone's duty living in Telos to serve at least one six-month term in the Silver Fleet. There are dozens of fleets that serve this sector of the galaxy. In our solar system, the fleets that are predominantly active are the Silver Fleet, the Amethyst Fleet and the Rainbow Fleet. Of these three, the Silver Fleet is made up almost exclusively of beings born on planet Earth, mostly from Telos and Posid *(the Atlantean city located under the Mato Grosso in Brazil)*.

The majority of scouts, more commonly known as the UFO's that you see in your skies, are Silver Fleet scouts from Telos and Posid. Many Telosians make a career out of serving in the Silver Fleet, while others just fulfill their obligation and go on to other service.

Another option at graduation is to begin training for your life's work in Telos. Young adults are expected to enter the general structure of the Telosian society. Everyone living in Telos, after a certain age, begins to participate in the daily workforce. Five days a week, four to six hours a day is dedicated to working; this is how the city keeps running. Everyone gets to choose where they want to place their energies, thus avoiding drudgery and creating enthusiasm instead. For example, if a young teen loves the earth, plants and flowers, he/she can work in the hydroponic gardens to help keep the city abundantly supplied with fruits and vegetables. If a young girl has a strong desire to become a dancer, she can go to the Temple to be trained by temple dancers. Other options include communications, transportation, cooking, manufacturing, household work, etc. At the age of eighteen our children begin their dance with life!

I am Adama, always at your side.

Chapter Eight

Temple of Union

Adama and Ahnahmar

Greetings and blessings, my beloveds, this is your friend
Adama. I am here today with Ahnahmar, one of our elders,
who has been living here since the beginning of our life
in Telos a little over 12,000 years ago. Ahnahmar lived in
Lemuria for over 2,000 years prior to the loss of our continent, and he has maintained the same youthful body for
about 14,000 years of your time. He is very tall, energetic
and handsome, and looks to be about 35 years of age or even
younger.

During the time of Lemuria, Ahnahmar and his twin flame
built a temple of wondrous beauty called "The Temple of
Union." This temple was built in honor of the Love and
Union of Twin Flames. Ahnahmar and his twin flame
have been the guardians of that unfed flame of Immortal
Love for the planet ever since. I now step back to allow
Ahnahmar to continue.

Greetings, I am Ahnahmar. Blessings and love to all those
who will read this message. In the time of Lemuria, most
men and women shared their lives with their beloved twin
flame. That majestic temple was the location for wedding
ceremonies. Couples adorned themselves in great beauty
and elegance to consecrate their "Union" with the energies

of the unfed flame of Immortal Love. Although this flame of Love was extinguished from the surface vibration with the sinking of Lemuria, it has been preserved in the Temple of Union which was lifted up in its entirety into the fourth dimension when our continent was destroyed.

This temple still exists today in the area near Mount Shasta where it was originally located, and is now vibrating at a fifth dimensional frequency. Although the former physical structure no longer exists in your third dimension and cannot be seen in your reality, be assured that it is very real and tangible to us. The temple is very active and continues to perform all the functions for which it was intended from the time it was built. This temple exists in the etheric crystal city of Light in the area of Mount Shasta. The city extends approximately 25 to 40 miles in diameter. You have been promised that this wondrous Lemurian city will eventually be lowered into a more physical expression and many of you will be able to see and enter it upon invitation. You are asking when this is going to happen. The exact time is still unknown, even to us. We anticipate that it will be towards the end of this decade or soon after. When this happens, the temple, along with all the other wonders of the crystal city, will be available to those who match the vibration in their spiritual development.

Aurelia, also known to you as Louise Jones, was involved with this temple in the time of Lemuria. She rediscovered the location of the temple a few years ago while taking walks close to her home in the Mount Shasta area. At first, she recognized that this was a very special place, but could not unveil the mystery. For reasons unknown to her consciousness, she felt drawn to return frequently to our area for walks and meditations. Several times a week we watched her walking up the hill, as she followed the nudging of her heart. It was always with delight and joy, especially the first time, that we watched her. We patiently waited for the day we could communicate with her more directly. Unknown to her outer mind, each time she came she received on the inner plane our warm welcome along with much attention, love and hugs from us.

It had been several thousand years since we had an opportunity to communicate consciously with any surface dweller in that location. There are those living in the area who come to the hill for walks from time to time, but none have been aware of what this location represents. More clarity was eventually offered to our dear Aurelia about the nature of her favorite location, and the strong attraction she felt. Her love and high degree of respect for the sacredness of that site allowed us to unveil ourselves to her more openly and reveal in greater measure details of her former involvement with us in this sacred temple.

In the fall of 2001, Aurelia performed a wedding ceremony in this location, consciously enrolling our full presence and the presence of the Light Realm. It was the first time since the sinking of Lemuria that a wedding ceremony had taken place in the physical octave directly within the location where our fifth dimension Temple of Union is situated. This was a most joyous moment for us, and we offered our full support. I, Ahnahmar, merged with my beloved Aurelia during the ceremony!

Unknown to her outer mind, Aurelia was preparing herself for a wonderful experience. Following her inner guidance, she suggested this special location to a twin flame couple who wanted her to officiate at their wedding ceremony. The Telosians, along with the Lemurian Council and the beings of the Light Realm, were very happy about this event. Literally hundreds of thousands of us, and millions from the invisible realm, attended this wedding in our etheric bodies. In a way, it was fortunate she could not see us because it could have been rather intimidating, considering the size of the crowd. It seems that everyone from Telos and the Light Realms of Mount Shasta were there, applauding the reactivation into the physical octave of the Flame of Love for Twin Flames from our temple.

It was only after the wedding that we revealed more information about the true nature of the temple and the wonderful activation that took place for the planet during the ceremony. By following her heart and inner guidance, we were amused to see how Aurelia provided the opportunity for us to create this wondrous opening into the physical plane. The scenario we had been waiting for unfolded in a perfect sequence, without her knowing what was really taking place besides a wedding ceremony. This too made us all smile.

Many of you have experienced marriage relationships as devastating, bringing more stress and disappointment than joy and sustained happiness. The reason is that stressful relationships are based on duality rather than the oneness of divine Love. Unless a relationship is based on oneness, it can never fulfill the longing of the heart that you feel so deeply.

Now, my friends, allow me to lecture you a little. As the guardian of the Unfed Flame of Love, I have observed your relationships for a long time. For those of you looking for your beloved somewhere outside yourself, let me say this is not the way it will happen. Your beloved is also part of you. He or she may have a body in the outer world, but meeting your twin flame when one is not fully ready for that initiation is a bit tricky. It is not often in your best interest because the experience of the third dimension does not always offer compatibility of character and spirit, unless both parties have reached the same level of readiness and evolution. Listen to this carefully.

Look for the love that you yearn for inside yourself first, in every cell and electron of your heart and soul. Begin first to develop a relationship in unity consciousness within yourself. It is all there awaiting your attention. Your divine counterpart lives within you. The relationship you seek is nothing more than the reflection of your direct relationship with your own divine Self. When you learn to love yourself in every aspect of your essence, every aspect of your divinity, every aspect of your human experience, then that divine love for Self becomes the ruler of your heart and life and you will no longer look anywhere else. You will know that you have found it and it will not really matter what form it takes. Your heart will feel full and completely satisfied.

At that stage of development in your spiritual life, the mirror or reflection of perfect love for Self will manifest itself tangibly in your life. This is divine law and cannot fail you. If it has not manifested in your life, either you are not ready for it or on the inner planes you have chosen to wait. It will show up in divine timing, and any waiting period will not matter because you will have united in your heart with the object of your yearning and your love. Once you have attained this state of divine love in your heart, nothing can be withheld from you, not even your twin flame.

In the name of divine love, may I suggest that you begin looking for your beloved within your Self. This is the quickest way to be united with your twin flame. You do not have to put ads in the paper or visit a singles club. He or she will literally fall into your lap; you will not be able to avoid it.

May you meet all your tests in the embrace of divine Love! It is my pleasure to invite you to come to my temple at night where I give classes for those desiring to reunite with their twin flame. I am not offering to become a matchmaker, as you call it. We are willing to assist you in reconnecting with that wondrous aspect of Self that you abandoned a long time ago, the very aspect that magnetizes your beloved and everything else you desire to you. We will not magnetize your beloved for you, but we will show you how to accomplish this for yourself. We will teach you the true meaning of "Divine Union."

Before you go to sleep at night, ask your guides to bring you to the Temple of Union to attend our classes. My fellow teachers and I will be there to receive you. I promise that we will have a delightful time together. If you do not remember your journeys with us, do not worry. With the thinning of the veils, many more of you will eventually open to the remembrance of your many delightful nightly adventures.

I am Ahnahmar, the guardian of the Temple of Union and the Unfed Flame of Immortal Love.

Marriages in Telos

***Many of you wonder about how we view our
romantic relationships in Telos and if we
have marriages and families like yours.***

Since we live very long lives and the potential for large families is great, careful planning for the benefit of all is of utmost importance. Unlike surface folks, no one is allowed to start a family in Telos until they have gained the maturity and the readiness to initiate such an important step.

***We do not allow children to give birth to children,
so to speak, like you do in the third dimension.***

We have two different types of marriage in our society. The first one is a "bonded" marriage. Two people who are attracted to each other romantically decide to unite in a bonded marriage union that is not necessarily permanent. They get married and live together to learn from and with each other, to grow in maturity together, to experience life and to enjoy each other to the fullest. They do this only as long as they are both deeply happy and satisfied with the relationship. There is no obligation for them to stay together, and these unions are not necessarily a lifetime commitment.

Couples engaged in a bonded marriage are not allowed to have children. The raising of children is not the primary goal of these marriages. These marriages can last anywhere from a few short years to several hundred years or longer. Birth control is not an issue for us. The birth of a child is considered a very precious and grand event for the incoming soul, and a child is conceived by "invitation" only. We have no such thing as an unwanted pregnancy in our society. A woman in Telos would get pregnant only by intention, and only after serious and well-planned preparations. Sexual unions alone do not manifest pregnancy unless the invitation to a specific soul exists. What you are dealing with in your society with unwanted pregnancies through sexual union is the result of a distorted genetic mutation. This too will heal in time when your DNA coding becomes fully restored by the embracing of unconditional love of self and of all life forms.

In a "bonded" marriage, couples may end their relationship at any time, without hurt feelings or obligations toward each other, and then start another one if they wish. This way, no one stays in a relationship for the wrong reason like you do in your society. Every couple in Telos is happy because there is no reason to stay together unless there is a deep love and satisfaction to be with each other. These marriages are considered part of the many experiences that life and evolution offer. When a couple feels they have come to the completion of their time together, they thank each other for the time they have spent together on the path of life and they move on, always remaining good friends. All they need to do is apply to the Lemurian Council of Telos for dissolution of their marriage and it is granted without any dispute.

It would be unthinkable for any of us to consider staying in a relationship unless there is total harmony, fulfillment and deep purpose.

Our second type of marriage is a "committed" or "sacred"

marriage. It is only in this type of marriage that couples are permitted to have children and apply to bring a new soul into the community. After a couple has been involved in a "bonded" marriage for several decades or a few hundred years, they may decide that they have experienced each other long enough to know with absolute certainty that their love for each other is flawless and long-lasting. They may then wish to make a lifetime commitment to each other.

Since we have become immortal, a lifetime commitment for us would normally mean a very long time in our society, extending into thousands of years. In a committed marriage there is no longer the option of dissolution of the marriage, or what you term divorce. For this reason, a couple already in a bonded marriage for a long time has to be very sure of their commitment to each other before they choose to engage in what is considered a permanent relationship. They stay together until such a time as one of them or both are ready to move on to a higher realm of evolution or service. In this case, one or both would leave Telos. This would happen only after a long life together and after the original family has matured through several generations.

In this type of marriage, one, two or sometimes three children may be born. The gestation period for the mother-to-be is only 12 weeks. Since the couple has already lived together a long time in a bonded marriage, they have accomplished whatever they wanted to experience together as a couple. They are now ready for the next step and have gained enough maturity and know-how to be accorded the privilege and honor of starting a family.

Only to our more mature and more evolved people is the privilege of bringing forth children granted, giving birth to noble and more advanced souls, thus perpetuating an enlightened civilization.

In our society, we have no orphans, nor children who are

abandoned or raised with the difficulties a single parent has to face in your society. Our family life is so carefully and wisely planned that our children never have to suffer such traumas as being unwanted, neglected or abused. We have no children struggling to raise children. Each child is considered a precious gift from God, loved and honored not only by the parents, but also by the whole of our community. Our civilization is fully aware of the sacredness of the role of bringing forth children and this is never undertaken lightly or without appropriate training. We pray that on the surface, you will soon start to honor the raising of children in a more enlightened and responsible way.

Relationships and Sexuality in Telos

Adama, please talk about relationships between men and women in Telos. How is sexuality handled between people of Telos? How can people in the third dimension evolve toward these types of relationships?

Greetings, my beloveds,

It is a real delight for me and for my team to be spending time with you in your energy field as you read our words. It is our most heart-felt desire to impart a greater understanding of divine laws and their applications for you.

The way we live our lives in Telos does not differ greatly from any other galactic community in this solar system or this universe. We are all living and applying the universal laws which are the same for everyone. How life is expressed from civilization to civilization may vary to a greater or lesser degree, but the core principles are the same for everyone. You may call it "unity or universal consciousness."

Our relationships and sexual expression in Telos reflect a

consciousness much more evolved and mature than yours in the understanding of the various applications of Love. To begin with, the curriculum for relationships is "union" in oneness, in an embrace of the experience of divine love. For a very long time in your dimension, relationships have been based on duality consciousness. Now dear ones, you have become weary of these types of relationships that do not work and do not fulfill your heart's desires.

Your relationships, for the most part, have caused you various levels of pain and longing. You are now yearning to gain a greater understanding of relationship. Many of you are waking up to the distorted programming you hold about relationships and seeking to balance the masculine and feminine energies within your being.

First of all, know that it all begins with you. Your "significant other" is simply a mirror for you to evolve with and learn from. No one can love you more than you love yourself, nor can you love someone else more than you love yourself. Consider this:

> *Whenever you are looking for someone to give you the love that you are not willing to give to yourself, you create need.*

You must embody the appropriate balance to attract the type of relationship you yearn for or the relationship will be based on neediness rather than oneness. This, my friends, will never work, at least not for very long. Remember that in an unsatisfying relationship, both partners mirror for each other the imbalances of neediness, of ownership, of unrealistic expectations, control, manipulation and so on. You know the entire litany of complaints about relationships in your dimension even better than we do.

Whenever people are whole and complete within Self, with balanced feminine and masculine energies, they are in love with themselves and do not need someone else to fulfill them emotionally. They feel whole, happy and successful. They exude the joy of life with or without a partner. They do not feel the emptiness within that being needy and out of balance produces.

When this balance is achieved, then and only then will the "I AM" of your being issue the call for the right relationship to appear in your life in alignment with your desire and your present pathway. This "divine union" with the twin flame of your heart can manifest in your life only by the permission of your Higher Self.

> ***In Telos we honor ourselves such that none of us would ever accept or settle for a relationship that is less than 100% fulfilling on all levels.***

In our society, we consider each other equals and we honor each other's divinity and soul path. Though your society is gradually changing, and women are now opening to their feminine potential as equal partners, there are still too many women who tolerate inequality as well as verbal and physical abuse. Too many of you do not yet feel worthy of being loved and you tolerate beatings, deprivation, and violation of your integrity and freedom. Too many of you still think that this is what you deserve, or you perceive abusive relationships as a normal way of life. Even in the USA, this consciousness still exists for many. It exists even more tragically in several countries on this planet where women have absolutely no rights. You know what and where I mean; you have seen it in your newspapers and television news.

In our society, and in all evolved societies, men and women consider each other as two aspects of God. The woman represents the aspects of the divine mother and the man represents the divine father. There is honor and respect between couples at all times. This does not mean that they always agree, but even when there is a difference of desire or perspective, they honor each other's viewpoint and do not fight or argue over it. They do not have this kind of attachment to being right or wrong, and they do not love each other any less because of their differences of perspective.

Couples spend as much time together as they wish. They have all the time they want to nurture, love and show their appreciation for each other as partners. Because we work approximately 20 hours a week, and the rest of the time we are free to use our time as we wish, couples have much time to enjoy each other's company in their homes and in the many social and artistic gatherings in our community. They are never short of time to nurture each other in many creative ways. They love to lavish each other with little attentions, tenderness and affection. They express their sexuality and intimacy with each other when they choose, always in a beautiful, relaxed atmosphere.

Relationships in Telos are not subject to the physical hardships of survival and the financial difficulties that you have to deal with in your society. Relationships between men and women do not have the same level of stress, and it is easier for couples to be consistently loving and harmonious. Because of our love, our mature consciousness and our honoring of the Earth, there is a constant flow of supply from the universe to fulfill our needs. This is what you are moving toward in the very near future.

We do not have to earn money to pay rent or feed the children, or pay medical bills or taxes. All commodities of life are free for everyone. The tyranny of earning money in your world will soon come to an end, hopefully within the next 10 to 12 years, and your overall stress will diminish greatly.

Tell us about relationships of young adults and teenagers.

Experimental relationships are also permitted when our

young people reach a certain age and their sexual hormones become active. We do not force them to suppress these natural desires. When they reach the age of thirteen or fourteen they are allowed to experiment with sexuality with each other under the supervision of the priesthood. These wise teachers prepare our youth to express their sexuality with maturity and responsibility. They are then allowed to go out on their own and experience what they have been taught. Their sexuality is always expressed with pure joy and delight in each other. Eventually, their youthful need to experience with more than one partner diminishes until there is the mature desire for commitment. In this way, our young adults in Telos are free to experiment with their sexuality as part of their maturing process.

There comes a time when two souls who wish to unite choose to make a commitment. It is usually a commitment for greater growth, not necessarily with the goal of permanence. When two souls wed in a committed marriage, they honor each other as part of the divine whole. Rarely do these relationships experience much stress, and may last from several years to several hundred years.

If or when both parties feel completion in their experience together, they part in a very friendly and loving manner, and in the harmony of mutual agreement. They say to each other: "Thank you, my dear. It was wonderful to have had this opportunity for growth with you. Thank you for the love, the tenderness and the affection we have shared, and for the spiritual growth and the wisdom we have gained. We shall remain friends as we each go our separate ways to our next experience of life and soul evolution."

Partners in Telos are very loving toward each other. When two souls are in a committed marriage for a long time experiencing great love for one another after hundreds or thousands of years together, they are usually twin flames. Sooner or later, the couple applies to the Lemurian Council for permission to enter into a sacred marriage. These unions are permanent and remain together as long as they both live in this dimension.

Tell us how partners express their sexuality in Telos.

In a sense, our bodies are not as physically dense as yours, and we can merge with each other in a much deeper and more intimate way. When we unite, we merge our physical bodies as well as our chakras in a union of love. We regard the sexual act as "a union with the divine" and all of our chakras participate, always in alignment with the heart, which brings a much expanded experience. Our sexual expression is based on engaging the fires of the heart first.

In your sexual expression on the surface, you mostly engage only the first two chakras of creativity and survival. For those really "in love" with each other, you engage the heart chakra as well. In Telos, we would never engage in a sexual act for the purpose of gaining favors or for manipulative reasons.

Because of our level of evolution, we have many more chakras activated than you do. We have twelve main chakras fully activated, as well as each of their twelve sub-chakras. This means 144 chakras are engaged in our sexual expression. When two people merge together as the divine feminine and the divine masculine in an expression of divine love, the energy of union resonates through the whole solar system. It is felt by the Father-Mother God. It becomes an act of the union of hearts merging with the Creator energy. This is how we view our sexuality.

Distorted sexual practices

For a long time, we have watched your sexual expressions, from the highest to the lowest in vibration. We encourage you to re-evaluate the negative emotional repercussions of sexual encounters holding little or no love for the other. There are still countries where a woman's clitoris is removed when she is very young to ensure that she will never experience any sexual pleasure, her goddess aspect totally denied. In entire cultures, women have been denied sexual pleasure by the male energy, and by those who have manipulated your planet's genetics by mixing sexuality with pregnancy.

Let me add something else. So many women on this planet have turned off their sexuality and their goddess energies because they have been abused, misused, desecrated, violated, repressed and dishonored. In past ages, women in general felt that they were of little value beyond service as a sex object or a material possession for men's physical and emotional needs. It is now time for both genders to heal those deep-seated wounds.

The Bringing Forth of Children

We are totally free to enjoy our sexuality without the burden or apprehension of unwanted pregnancies. Pregnancies manifest only when a soul is invited by intention to evolve in our community. The pregnancy then takes place energetically in the subtle body and manifests physically. Only in sacred marriages are couples allowed to bring forth children. When a couple makes a decision to have a child, they go to the temple to discuss their intention with the head priest and apply for permission to receive this privilege. Only couples who have attained high spiritual maturity are allowed to bring forth souls into incarnation. This is the way it is in all enlightened civilizations.

When permission is granted for a couple to bring forth a new soul into our community, it is considered a very sacred calling. The parents-to-be are then in direct connection with one or more candidates from the light realm for that special privilege. Once the candidate is chosen, many meetings take place at an inner level between the incoming soul and the future parents. There is approximately six to twelve months of preparation for conception. Soul path and purposes are studied carefully until all is in readiness for that sacred commitment.

It would be unthinkable in our society to bring a child into incarnation without first implementing the highest and most complete preparations.

We are totally aware of the impact the birth of a new soul will create in our community. When the soul is conceived, the gestation period is twelve weeks. The parents temporarily move to the temple for full-time preparation for the event. During that time, the parents-to-be lavish each other with the purest love they are capable of as a couple. They listen to music that elevates their vibration and surrender themselves into exquisite beauty. The members of the temple priesthood honor and welcome the soul who is destined to become part of our community. Our children are always wanted and desired. During the gestation period, the soul waiting to be born feels fully the love of the parents and of the community.

Our children are born slightly larger than yours and they grow more rapidly; they also grow in wisdom and knowledge. Though they may experience some of the difficulties children do on the surface, especially at puberty, we have many ways to assist them to mature and grow through their problems. Each child's pathway is always honored, and each child receives all the attention he/she requires.

Is there anything that you can share with those of us in the third dimension on how we can evolve into the same state of consciousness?

Well, it is coming, dear one. It is coming with increased

awareness and awakened consciousness. Those who are reading our information are grasping the meaning and want to create this kind of life for themselves. They want to live in this kind of enlightened society. As you are aligning with these principles of higher consciousness, you are also creating it. It will evolve in the coming years. In the near future, more and more people will open their consciousness to the information we are sharing. As this number increases, you will see things start to change rather rapidly.

You know that intentions create reality. When enough people desire change and formulate firm intentions to create a new reality for themselves and for humanity, it will simply happen. It is important at this time that each one of you becomes an ambassador of love, peace and harmony for yourself, for humanity and for the planet. It is important that you begin sharing the information that you feel makes a difference in your lives with those around you.

> ***The time to be silent in your cocoon is over.***
> ***You all need to shine your love, your light, and***
> ***your knowledge to all of those on your pathway.***

The more you shine and radiate your new understanding, the more it will expand within you and the planet. This is how evolution moves on. We have noticed among the people of the French population who have read our books, that there has been quite a shift in awareness and a substantial increase of desire for enlightened living. We have also noticed men and women honoring each other more. Everyone will have to start embracing their divinity and balancing their polarities whether they are in a male or a female body. Do you understand that? When you are aligned with your inner polarities and you meet someone who is similarly aligned, you will begin living new experiences in relationships that will bring you much greater satisfaction.

Right knowledge and information create food for the soul

that brings transformation. As more people become aware and open their hearts to these concepts, the hundredth-monkey effect will reach the mass consciousness. Watch for the leaps in consciousness and life-style that people on this planet will embrace in a few years time.

The greater the number of people who embrace this type of information, the faster higher consciousness will evolve for humanity. These concepts of divine law are now in an embryonic state in the heart of the few. As you share your new discoveries with those who are open to it, they will germinate and grow. Once enough people hold the desire in their heart for this kind of leap in consciousness, you will not be able to stop the growth from taking place. It is just a question of informing a sleeping population through writings and teachings, and bringing recognition of the truths that have been hidden from you for so long.

As the population wakes up to their spiritual destiny, you will experience a tremendous acceleration of light for manifesting the promised Golden Age of Love, Peace, Enlightenment and Prosperity for all in your world.

Begin to consider your bodies
As "magical forms."
See them as the most versatile machines
That were ever created
That can do all you want them to do
Without pain or limitation.
- Adama

Learn the lessons of harmlessness—
Neither by word, nor thought, nor feeling
Will you ever inflict evil or harm
Upon any part of life.
Know that action and physical violence
Will keep you in the realm of pain,
Suffering and mortality.
-Maha Chohan, Paul the Venetian

Chapter Nine

The Animals in Telos

***In Telos, we have many species of
animals we saved from extinction.***

When we knew our continent was going to be destroyed
and we built our underground city to preserve our lives
and all ancient records of our civilization, we also saved
a few of every species of animal in existence at the time.
In this regard, we can be compared to an earlier, but expanded version of the biblical story of Noah, who saved in
his Ark two members of every species prior to the sinking
of Atlantis. Most of these are alive and in our care to this
day, except for those that have chosen, as a species, to return to their place of origin. The demise of Lemuria came
about 1,200 years prior to the sinking of Atlantis, and at
that time many species of animals present prior to the
destruction of our continent were already extinct from the
surface.

***We say to you that animals embody
again and again, just like you do.***

Their embodiments are always extensions of a much larger
whole. All of us, including animals, are extensions of a
vast Being of Light, so vast and so wondrous that you
will stand in absolute amazement the day you open to the

understanding of your true Divinity. The concept of multi-dimensionality remains very difficult to fully comprehend within the limitations of a third dimensional mind. God, in his beingness and true nature of Love, is constantly creating and forever extending and expanding Himself in a wider and wider spectrum and variety of manifestation. The animal kingdom is just one among many of these infinite expansions. All are part of God, dear ones, ALL.

When you allow yourself to hurt one part of Life (God), you are hurting the whole, including yourself.

On the Inner Planes, all animals have great intelligence, and are not accurately represented in your current awareness. Some of them rule worlds and planets. Animals live in many dimensions. All animals have an over-soul or a higher self, as humans do, but it is of a slightly different nature. They are created as part of a kingdom that is not the same as your kingdom. Thus, they are also extensions of a much larger body of consciousness, another aspect of Divinity.

Consciousness extends itself from the highest levels of the Godhead to the lowest level of the first dimension of rocks and minerals. All are God in various expressions.

The higher the dimension, the greater is the understanding of Love and the more expanded is the awareness. Animals share your planet with you because, like you, they have chosen to come here to experience the third dimension. They have also come as helpers and teachers to assist mankind in ways you do not yet understand. Just because they chose to come in a body that differs from yours does not make them inferior to you. Even if they were, there is no moral or spiritual justification for the way many animals are presently treated on the Earth's surface. Their bodies are just an overtone lower than yours in third dimensional expression.

***There is not the difference you have been taught
to believe for so long. Many humans on
the surface have used this excuse as a
passport for animal exploitation.***

In your limited understanding, you have allowed yourself to see many species of animals as commodities to be used for selfish means or profit. The golden rule needs to be applied for all sentient beings, not just for the human kingdom. In order to move forward on the platform of your own evolution, you must offer unconditional love in words, thoughts, feelings and deeds toward all life forms and all kingdoms living on this planet. This is the only way, because love is the main key.

***There is not an atom of creation that
has not manifested through Love.***

There is not an atom of creation that you can choose "not to love" if you wish to move forward. In the spirit world, animals function at the fourth and fifth dimensional levels. They are all connected to a higher body of Light. All humans are connected to their own Higher Selves, their God Presence, existing in higher dimensions and living in each heart.

The Higher Self of your being, your own God Presence, is a glorious, intelligent, powerful being of unlimited perfection and splendor. Your third dimensional life on Earth reflects only a small portion of the totality of your Divinity.

In creation and in the Higher Realms, there is no such thing as lesser, lower, better than or not so good as, etc. These are all labels of limited human awareness. All are equally loved and considered expressions of God in constant motion *(evolution)*. There is a difference between you and the animals, but it is not what you have been led to believe. My friends, in the subterranean cities, we have much respect for animals and we consider them as our younger brothers and sisters on the ladder of evolution.

We treat animal life with the same consideration and love we would like to receive for ourselves.

Let's say that in a human family, for example, there are ten children. Would you say that the younger ones are inferior to the older ones just because they have less life experience, and do not yet know as much as the older ones? Would you say that the younger ones do not deserve to be treated with as much love and consideration because they were born later than the others, or that they can be abused just because they are not yet as developed as the older ones?

I would think not. You know very well that in a few years they will catch up. So it is, my friends, with the animals. In the hierarchy or family of the body of the One God, the animals, who share our planet, are the younger members. It is my expectation that you will understand the point I am trying to make. Everything in creation has consciousness, from the greatest to the smallest. Ultimately, all are considered equal.

As I mentioned before, we have in our care in Telos a large number of species of animals that have been extinct from Earth's surface for a very long time. Other civilizations who have been underground longer than we also hold in their care large numbers of animal species that have been extinct from the surface for even longer. We have many species of cats. Their sizes vary from five to six pounds to several hundred pounds. We have species of dogs and horses that are more evolved than the ones you know on the surface, and will bring you much delight when they are eventually allowed to emerge among you.

Most of our animals are larger than the ones you now have. For example, many of the big cats are almost twice the size of the ones on the surface. Many horses are larger, but some have retained a size that you will really be able to enjoy.

Our animals are very dear to us. Be assured that they will not be released into your hands until violence is totally eliminated from your world.

All of our animals are gentle and have never been exposed to negativity or violence of any sort. Anyone can walk up to them in total safety and cuddle with them, including large cats that weigh several hundred pounds. None of our animals have any fear of humans; neither do they kill or eat each other. They are all vegetarians. Our animals have never been hunted or caged. They are allowed to live their full life-span, which is much longer than surface animals.

Be assured that we will not take the chance of releasing any of them into surface civilizations as long as there is the slightest possibility for them to be hurt or receive less love than they are accustomed to. We recognize the unique intelligence each species of animal arrives with and we have no need ever for them to be submissive. They are docile and willing to please.

Telepathic communication is all that is needed for us to have total cooperation from any animal.

On behalf of all civilizations of the Earth Within, I say to you that it is with great joy and anticipation that we will watch all of you, our dear brothers and sisters, as you open your minds, hearts and souls to the animal kingdom, and begin changing the way you have perceived and treated them.

We send you our Love, our Light and our Friendship. We very much look forward to the time of our emergence to the surface, to be with you again, to shake your hands and to teach you what we have learned from living for thousands of years in the vibration of Love, Peace and Brotherhood, free of war, control, greed, fear, manipulation and endless bureaucracy.

***Together, we will forge a very bright future
for all citizens of the New Earth.***

When we emerge from our subterranean abodes, through the maze of tunnels leading to every country and city on the planet, it will be a time of great rejoicing for all those who open their hearts and minds to receive us. We are your senior brothers and sisters and we love you all very dearly.

Chapter Ten

Questions and Answers

Interventions from Other Races

**We hear that sometimes the Inner Earth beings
intervene in events taking place in our society.
How and when is that decision made,
and who does the intervention?**

Inner Earth beings are not allowed to intervene in the affairs of the surface dimension, or to interfere with the free will of humanity. We are members of the Galactic Confederation of Planets and under the direction of The Council of Twelve. When intervention on the surface of this planet is needed, this council is in control. We would or could intervene only at their request and with their full authorization. This does not mean that we have never intervened in any way, but we want you to understand that until now, until the "Grand Experiment" on planet Earth is over, it is not appropriate for us to interfere with the free will choices of humanity. We have not interfered with the sinking of two major continents, nor have we interfered with all the wars and devastation you have chosen to initiate.

The Divine intervention this planet is about to experience is indeed an intervention directly called forth by your Creator. Because of this, countless extraterrestrials from millions of star systems, your Space Brothers, who love you so very much, are now here by the billions to prepare for and to assist you and your planet during the "Great Shift." Among the many various ET civilizations here to help are the Arcturians, the Pleiadeans, the Andromedans, the Sirians, the Venusians, those from Alpha Centauri, the positive Nibirians and Orions, and many others.

The Space Brothers, whom many of you long to reconnect with tangibly, are members of your soul family. They are friends and family of your "future selves." They have often intervened by protecting the Earth from major space disasters that could have caused much destruction. Unknown to you, they have protected the Earth and all of you many, many times from major invasions by space cultures who have not yet learned to embrace unconditional love and true brotherhood. The Arcturians, the Sirians, the Pleiadeans and many others have been your most devoted Space friends and guardians. They are still here at this time in great numbers to assist you and to stabilize your planet during the coming changes and dimensional shifts. They send you love every day.

It is with a great deal of sadness that we observe how you treat your planet and each other, as members of God's family. The only intervention that beings who live within the Earth have been allowed is to send you Love and Light, and to comfort you when you are in pain, sadness and sorrow. For eons, from the other side of the veil, all from the Earth's interior have guided and instructed you. We have shared our wisdom, our grace, our love and the workings of true brotherhood for peace and prosperity with you. We have worked with you in your dream state and between your incarnations. Again and again, for millennia, prophets, great sages and avatars were sent to you. Unfortunately, most were ignored, persecuted or very often killed.

There was an agreement made a long time ago between the

Inner Earth people and the collective of souls evolving on the surface dimension of the planet that your experiments with separation were to be "hands off." The way you had chosen to evolve and learn your lessons was not to be interfered with. The same with your Earth Mother; she has allowed you all your choices at the expense of the comfort and beauty of Her own body. She allowed all your choices until the day it was decreed by the Prime Creator that, "the Great Experiment on Earth is now over." This day, my friends, has come. The decree from your Creator for your re-awakening and the restoration of your divinity, has been heard throughout this entire universe and beyond. All on Earth are now in intensive preparation for the "Great Reunion" and the "Great Shift." It is time to go forward; do not seek to go back. Let go of the old to embrace the New World.

Crop Circles

It has been said that people in the Inner Earth participate in the making of crop circles. Is it a joint venture with the extraterrestrials? Will crop circles eventually become permanent? If so, what will be their role?

Crops circles are mainly fourth and fifth dimensional gardens. They are indeed created in cooperation with Inner Earth people, extraterrestrials and the devic consciousness, but they are mainly the work of extraterrestrials. They are temporarily created in your third dimension to wake up your curiosity to assist you in expanding your mind and to open up a new way of thinking for you. It is time to embrace a much larger picture of Creation and the Universe. These crop circles are encoded with sound and light emanations that will assist in the re-awakening of your soul and divine consciousness.

Consider the beautiful gardens you will create in your

future to match the beauty of your new homes. Compare them to crop circles. In the not-so-distant future, what you now call a crop circle, a strange phenomena, will become so familiar to you that it will no longer be considered unusual. They are the beautiful gardens of your future, full of light, color and sound. You will be creating, with your intentions, awesome gardens similar to crop circles in frequency and encoding. You will put into these gardens whatever you wish; whatever your creativity can conceive of will manifest almost effortlessly. These gardens will continuously replenish themselves with blooms and fruit until you decide you want something else, and then your new creation will quickly manifest.

Crop circles are presented to you now for your pleasure, and to give you a glimpse of your future. Open your heart and mind to all the wonders that are ahead of you after the Earth's purification.

Crystals

What will be the role of crystals in the years to come?

Crystals have many forms, vibrations and dimensions. Crystals also have their own form of intelligence and awareness. They evolve and grow to be of service to you, especially when you are in your divine consciousness. What you know and have seen of crystals in your third dimensional awareness is very limited.

In the fourth and fifth dimension, crystals are lighter, clearer, and more luminous because they are able to absorb and contain much more light than the ones you presently know. They will take any form, size, vibration and color to meet your needs. You will be able to manifest them at will. You will no longer have to pay an exorbitant amount of money to acquire them. They will manifest according to your level of Love and Light and your right use of God's resources.

They will be the main source of energy used for the advanced technology that will be gifted to you when we come out of our cities in the Earth's interior. You will use them to travel anywhere in this universe, and to retrieve information from the Universal Mind. You will find that all of Earth's Living Library *(which is your complete story)* is stored in large crystal plates, rather than books, and you will have the technology to access any information very quickly from any location. The crystal grid of the Earth herself has already received an ascension activation, and this grid is now available to many for healing energies and information.

The "crystal children" incarnated in your world possess a direct connection in their DNA to communicate through this grid. You too have the option of opening to this form of consciousness, as do all who live on the surface during this time of Great Awakening and Shift. The shifts in the electromagnetic grid and the crystal grid have taken place to enable the greatest shift, that of human consciousness.

Instead of using wood, brick, cement or synthetic materials, you will use various types of crystalline structures to construct your private dwellings and public buildings. You will be living in homes that will appear to you as if you are living in crystal palaces, and yet you will still be able to maintain your privacy. These crystalline structures will reinforce your own energetic structure and support the many changes in your multi-dimensional DNA that signal your ascension to a fifth dimensional vibration and beyond.

As your own telepathic energies increase through activation of your own crystalline energy grid, you will no longer need physical crystals for communicating with each other around the planet. You will simply tap into the Earth's overall crystal grid and the etheric grid that encircles the planet. When you travel in space, those of you who have not yet attained the necessary level of universal telepathic skills will use crystals for inter-planetary and inter-galactic communications. In your spacecraft all communications systems will be crystalline-based. Your use of crystals and crystalline energy will become unlimited.

Guardians of Portals and Gateways

Can you address the subject of portals and gateways, and the beings who guard and regulate them?

In this short discourse, we can only touch briefly on a basic understanding of this topic. There is much more that is not appropriate for us to discuss with you at this time.

When you become curious about portals, it is a clear signal that you have a desire to expand your consciousness to a much greater understanding of the universe. There are a myriad of intricate complexities in the dimensions that exist beyond your third dimensional awareness. This includes gateways, energy vortexes, multi-dimensional corridors, planetary, galactic and universal grid systems, light barriers, time capsules, and many more concepts with which you are not yet familiar. They all work together as related components of a gigantic universal system. All of these concepts and realities, my friends, as well as the magic and wonder they inspire, will soon be yours to discover. You are now beginning to use some of them more consciously as you and the Earth evolve to higher frequencies and dimensions.

Since your question is about the guardians of those portals and gateways, I would like to explain the following in a simple manner. Portals, gateways and multi-dimensional corridors exist in great numbers from the highest level of the Godhead at the Universal Source, down through all created universes, all dimensions and sub-levels of each dimension, to the tiniest particle of life in the first dimension. They also exist throughout the great Void.

Portals and gateways are how God, or Source Energy, is disseminated throughout all of Creation. They are also the means by which Source Energy is stepped down from the universal levels to the galactic, solar system and planetary levels into all dimensions and life frequencies. There is great variety of portals, gateways and multi-dimensional corridors, each one fulfilling a specific function. For example, some portals are used for stepping down the frequency of Source Energy, while others are used for traveling between dimensions, planets, solar systems, galaxies, and universes. Each one of these billions of portals, gateways and corridors function with great mathematical accuracy so that chaos does not occur. This subject is so vast that only a small portion can be covered here, but I wanted to give you a broader awareness of what this subject entails, and how everything works together in great harmony and with ease and efficiency.

Who are the beings who guard and monitor these portals and gateways?

They are mainly evolved beings from the angelic kingdom, as well as those you call extraterrestrials. They have volunteered for these "jobs." Since they exist in great numbers in each group in the Light Realms, they take turns fulfilling these positions, thus avoiding drudgery for anyone at any time. These portals and corridors of Light are filled with various kinds of wondrous and interesting "comfort stations" of great beauty that cosmic travelers use to meet friends, to recharge their energies, or to simply receive information and direction. At times, they are the sites of great encounters between beings from many dimensions.

Following are a few guidelines for some of the portals for

this planet, solar system and galaxy. The same principles apply everywhere, but the higher you go in frequency, the more highly evolved are the guardians of these portals.

The first rule is that no one can travel freely through portals or gateways to dimensions higher than the level of consciousness they themselves have attained. You must first have the permission of those who reside where you want to go. Permission is sometimes granted to souls who are not yet at the necessary level if they are accompanied by a sponsor, a being from a higher dimension who accompanies them. A planetary ascended master who has attained a high level of consciousness may also volunteer to take such a soul to their destination.

For example, if you were personally called to the Great Central Sun of this Universe for an interview with the Father/Mother God, a being such as Sananda, Mother Mary or Saint Germain could take you there or an emissary from that plane would come to get you. In order to get there, you would have to travel through various multi-dimensional planetary, galactic and universal corridors and gateways. Unless you are with someone who has a cosmic passport to travel those corridors, you may not be allowed to go all the way to the Great Central Sun. The role of the guardians is to maintain the integrity and purity of the various planetary systems, galaxies and universes.

Each corridor, gateway, portal and grid system is guarded by beings who resonate with the level of frequency of the place they are protecting. Unless this resonance is matched, entry may be denied. These rules safeguard the integrity, purity and efficiency of those portals and corridors. Understand that if you were to travel to the Great Central Sun or the Galactic core through these corridors, it is a very great physical distance from the Earth plane. If I were to explain in detail all the steps, it would fill several chapters and you would see how complicated this becomes.

In reality, when one has attained the level of evolution that is required to travel to those places, it only takes seconds to arrive there. These corridors allow cosmic travelers to visit countless planets or galaxies and places beyond this universe. Your travel happens in the twinkle of an eye, unless you choose to make several stops along the cosmic highways to enjoy the view and social activities.

A long time ago, in our solar system and Milky Way galaxy, the Arcturians took on the job of creating and maintaining a large percentage of our multi-dimensional portals and corridors. They have become great experts in this work, and their expertise has been and will continue to be in demand throughout this entire universe. The role of the guardians of portals is to prevent unwanted energies from infiltrating places of great purity and wisdom. It is also to offer direction, guidance, comfort and information to travelers who are learning multi-dimensional travel and traveling those corridors for the first time. You may want to consider these guardians as "diplomatic relation teams."

Actually, none of this happens exactly the way I am explaining it to you now. The complexity simply cannot be explained and comprehended from a third dimensional perspective. This explanation will give you a basic idea, however, of how it works. Spacecraft also travel through those systems of corridors, gateways and grid systems to go wherever they want at great speed.

Although I mentioned that the Arcturians are the great masters and guardians of the main portals of this galaxy, they are not the only ones. Each planetary system has its own portal and corridor system that is guarded and maintained, usually by advanced souls from that same system. The Sirians and the Andromedans, among others, also work in close collaboration with the Arcturians to maintain these vast and numerous multi-dimensional openings.

Those of you who are star-seeds, who have come to this planet from other worlds, are already familiar with most of these portals, corridors and the Beings who guard them. When you are not in a physical body, you already know how to get back and forth. Once you have completed your evolutionary process here of ascension and enlightenment, you will remember how to do this quite easily. Your grand cosmic passport will be returned to you with the stamp for a much expanded arena of cosmic traveling than the one you previously were allowed. I promise that you will never be bored or weary again unto eternity. You will be free to join those who are busy exploring and expanding.

Chapter Eleven

We Have Immortalized Our Bodies

Adama

I am communicating with you from our fifth dimensional city within Mount Shasta. The Lemurian Council of Twelve of Telos and I would like to express our gratitude for this opportunity to commune with the many of you who read our message.

As we open wide our hearts to you, we ask you to open your hearts to us as well. We invite you to focus on communicating with us as often as you wish. We have the ability to bring much healing to the various aspects of your lives needing to come into greater balance. Be assured that we are always willing, able and ready to assist you in so many ways. By opening your heart and minds to us, we can assist you in the rapid transformation of your lives that otherwise might take much longer. We know that you all enjoy short-cuts, and interacting consciously with us will assist you in creating many shortcuts in your lives that will ease your burdens and accelerate your spiritual progress.

Many of you question if we are still physical like you in ways that can be seen and touched. Others argue that we are totally etheric, meaning that we no longer have bodies that are visually physical and tangible in your dimension. For the sake of clarity, let me explain that we have now evolved into beings that vibrate at a fifth dimensional frequency, with bodies that have attained a state of immortality and total perfection. We have chosen to retain enough density in them to remain visible and tangible when we choose to be, while experiencing no limitations of any kind. The original solar blueprint of our bodies is the same as yours.

Our DNA is also the same as yours was before you allowed yourself to mutate into the great density you have been experiencing on the surface for a very long time. Our DNA has continued to evolve, and our physical bodies no longer experience degeneration and aging. Although we feel as physical in our bodies as you do, lowering our frequency to the level of the third dimension is no longer comfortable for us.

> *Most of us have the ability to ride several dimensions at will, and this gives us much flexibility, freedom and delight.*

Our physical bodies have attained the level of perfection that you are all hoping for. Therefore, we function at a much higher frequency than you do. Our physical bodies function with the perfection that was always intended by our Creator. Basically, your bodies and our bodies have the same potential; they were created with the same divine blueprint.

This means, beloved ones, that in a few short years, as your awareness shifts from the limitations and judgments of the third dimensional frequency to the awareness and unconditional love of the fifth dimension, you will all learn to raise your bodies' frequency as we have. You will gradually experience the delights of seeing, feeling and experiencing your physical bodies transforming right in front of your eyes, increment by increment, within a relatively short time.

It will be unique for each person. You will release all the old limiting beliefs that have kept you in pain, suffering and lack. You will begin experiencing the rejuvenation of your body, which will function according to your original blueprint of solar perfection with many additional attributes.

For several golden eras, including the time of Lemuria, we all lived in a fifth dimensional awareness with bodies that could switch back and forth between the fifth and third dimensional frequencies. This was fun and exciting until a succession of events caused almost the entire Earth population to permanently focus on third dimension awareness. We were no longer able to reconnect with our fifth dimensional reality.

Soon, as you evolve your consciousness into the LOVE frequency and are able to maintain it there, your physical bodies will shed their present level of density. The former "magic" you once knew in the time of Lemuria will return for your enjoyment and exploration. Your bodies will become immortal and limitless again like ours.

And this time, dear ones, the magic will seem much greater because you have experienced your lives without it for so long and your lives have been very difficult. You have learned much since those gifts were lost to you. Because you have suffered for so long and have learned great soul lessons, you will never again take for granted the gift of immortality and divine perfection.

Your Physical Body Mirrors Your Consciousness

What will be the next discoveries in the Health Sciences? Do you intervene to guide our health practices?

We do not intervene into your health practices, your eating habits, the stressful lives you have chosen to embrace, your emotional overload, or your healing modalities. You came here to experience free will and we can only make suggestions as to the manner in which you choose to live your lives. Our approach to health, healing and aging is vastly different from yours.

First of all, none of us in Telos know any weakness or disease of any kind in our physical bodies. In our lives, we always apply divine principles to all we think, say and do. In our belief system, we know that our bodies were created as perfect and wondrous machines that were meant to live for thousands of years without any sign of weakness, aging or dying. This concept is completely natural to us because this is what everyone here experiences. All of our people can and do immortalize their physical bodies without much effort. We have fully embraced immortality and none of our people look to be over 40 years of age, though they may be 15,000 years old and more. Some of the folks in Telos are over 30,000 years of age but look to be 35. We have no hospitals, nursing homes, nurses, doctors, dentists, health insurance or anything of that kind.

When we eat, we eat only the purest, high-energy vibration food we can produce, totally organic and totally balanced with rich minerals that keep our bodies eternally strong and youthful. 98% of the food you eat is altered and made toxic with artificial chemicals such as preservatives, artificial food enhancers, herbicides, pesticides, ultra pasteurization, etc.

We would say that most of the food you eat is poorly grown and devoid of life force.

By the time you eat it, it is already old, altered and depleted of its natural nutrients and possesses little, if any, life force.

What you eat and how you eat it is not conducive to maintaining healthy, strong physical bodies in a state of immortality. Begin to read the ingredients on the labels of all food you put in your mouth and you will start noticing how artificial and synthetic your food is. As a rule, when reading ingredients on your food labeling, if you cannot read it easily, know what it is or pronounce it without hesitation, do not buy it.

We monitor what you feed your bodies on a daily basis and are astonished that you are not in worse health, considering the way you feed and treat your bodies. The creation of your physical bodies is so awesome; we remind you not to take them for granted. Your physical body is your tool of evolution for your incarnation. It is your holy temple and you should consider it worthy of the greatest care and love.

The illnesses or diseases you are experiencing with your physical bodies are nothing more than mirrors of your life-styles and consciousness.

For us, the way you eat and live would be a death trap. Unfortunately, this is what most of you accept without question and consider normal on the surface. You do not need a scientist or health department to make so called "health discoveries." You need consciousness awakening and deep appreciation of your physical bodies.

No wonder your bodies start aging shortly after the age of 30 years. No wonder that by the time you reach 60 or sooner, most of you are plagued with several health problems, and you are looking forward to living on your retirement check or social security. The majority of the surface population do not live past the age of 90.

The constitution of your bodies is already weakened at birth by generations upon generations of poor eating habits, stressful lives and mandatory vaccinations. Your bodies never receive the kind of quality food that will sustain them in harmony.

Why do you neglect your body and deprive it of what it needs to remain vibrant, healthy and youthful?

Why not cherish your bodies and give them what they really need instead of looking to some other source to provide you with band-aid solutions that are so very temporary? There is no real healing outside of self. It all starts with your level of consciousness and belief system. It is best that you make your own discoveries when it comes to nourishing and nurturing your bodies. Notice, I use the word nurturing. Yes, your bodies, especially on the surface, require much more nurturing and loving than you presently give yourselves.

Return to nature, dear ones; it will not fail you. Your emotional overload also affects deeply the state of your physical wellness. Your lack of exercise, lack of fresh air, the level of toxicity that many of you subject the body to at work and your stress level all contribute to the breakdown of your bodies. Thousands of you in America and world-wide, work in airtight buildings, breathe recycled air all day long while your bodies sit in front of a computer and /or a desk with a telephone in your hands. By the time you come home, you are too tired to exercise or make a "real meal" for yourselves, and rely too often on lifeless processed microwaved dinners.

In addition, have a look at the liquids you put into your mouths. You drink almost exclusively waters containing harmful substances such as synthetic chlorine, fluoride and other water decontamination chemicals. 95% of your water comes out of pipes and is contaminated in many ways. Check where your water source comes from and what is done to it to make it supposedly "safe" and drinkable. Though these waters may be considered safe and drinkable by your standards, they no longer hold any healing or rejuvenation energies.

Think of how much coffee, soda, beer and alcohol of all kinds and other synthetic drinks are sold and consumed around the world each day. Your bodies need to be cleansed and purified on a regular basis. Pure, crystalline, "non-adulterated" water is what is required for you to drink daily in order to maintain your body in a constant state of wellness.

> ***All illnesses and diseases are caused by the same things, no matter what names they are given by your medical authorities!***

They are caused by genetic, nutritional, mental and emotional imbalances and toxicity. All this can be changed quite easily with a little more enlightenment and willingness to honor your body and your incarnation. The labels that your medical establishment gives diseases are relative. They only represent the acknowledgement of how those imbalances personally manifest themselves in your bodies.

The greatest health discovery we predict you will make in the next few years is the "awareness" that you can change all your eating habits, start exercising more, have more fun, reduce your physical and emotional stress level, and let go of old beliefs that keep you sick and tired. You will discover a more holistic and integrated way of life that will be much more conducive to keeping your bodies in perfect health at all times for as long as you choose. True healing, dear ones, can only come from the soul and consciousness. Outside modalities are always secondary, and their benefits can only reflect the internal changes you are making.

> ***I will conclude the answer to this question by saying that your physical body mirrors your consciousness. In this incarnation on Earth, you live in a "house of mirrors."***

As you heal your emotions, love yourself unconditionally, open up to the ways of higher consciousness and apply these laws in your daily life, your body will reflect those changes and be transformed. The old saying: "Man, Heal Thyself" is indeed the wisdom you will discover.

How to Raise One's Consciousness

How to raise one's consciousness is a broad subject, dear ones, which could fill an encyclopedia. The answer to this question is like a diamond with several thousand facets, each facet representing an avenue in which you raise your consciousness above and beyond your present understanding of what life is about on this planet.

Before you would want to raise your consciousness, perhaps you would ask yourself a few questions such as:

- What does it mean to raise my consciousness?

- Why would one want to do this?

- What happens when one raises his/her consciousness?

- How will it affect my present life?

- What could be the results of such a spiritual journey, that literally never ends ... unto eternity?

- What does it mean to embrace one's divinity fully?

When you begin contemplating the answers to these questions deeply in your heart, you will have already begun the process. Your own GodSelf will step in with your willingness and will send you promptings and guidance to assist you with the process. Remember it is a process, dear ones, unfolding increment by increment according to your own unique pathway and the level of action and intensity you are investing in your healing process.

104

Once you develop a more expanded understanding of the questions above, raising your consciousness will become so much easier. You can make a fun game of unlimited discoveries out of it, a "Voyage in Self Discovery."

Let me give you a brief answer for each one of these questions. I leave you with the homework of expanding these concepts a thousand times, not so much in your mind, but mainly in the heart. Your heart, your sacred heart, my beloveds, is the supreme intelligence of your soul.

What does it mean to raise or expand one's consciousness?

It means to start becoming more conscious at all levels and in all aspects of your life. No more living on automatic pilot, and no more giving your power away to others. This means opening up step-by-step to your divinity, to the wondrous spiritual being you are in the midst of living your chosen human experience, chosen before your incarnation for the lessons you desired to learn in this present life.

It means to stop the madness in your life, at least for a period of time each day, in meditation or contemplation for the purpose of exploring the "Real Self." Begin opening yourself to all possibilities. Explore the wonders and the glory that are contained within you and around you, in nature and everything you see, feel and touch. Explore the intricacies and complexities of other kingdoms on this Earth that you have never paid attention to before. Explore within your heart and discover the golden angel that is your true Self, another aspect of your eternal identity.

Start exploring the vastness, the wonders of Love and Patience of the being you call Mother Earth. As you begin honoring yourself, also honor Her and Her body, as She is one who can assist you mightily in raising your consciousness and vibration.

Begin now the most wondrous journey of self-discovery and claim your true nature, as an unlimited divine being having a temporary human experience.

Why would I want to raise my consciousness?

The human experience on Earth has been difficult and full of challenges for the last several thousands of years, primarily because of the dense level of consciousness of you surface dwellers. You have allowed yourselves to gradually descend from the heights of the glory of higher consciousness in the first three golden ages, to your present way of life that does not outpicture the divine being you are. For the great majority, your way of life is not natural to your soul. In general, humans have lost contact with and forgotten their divine nature. In many ways, you still worship a God outside of yourself.

As you raise your consciousness again to the level of your Godhood, embracing your divinity in its fullness, all gifts of your divine birthright will be restored. You will again be able to demonstrate in daily life the ease, magic and grace of the unlimited God being you truly are. You will raise yourself forever above the pain and suffering of the present limitations you have lived with.

What happens when one raises their consciousness?

It will be helpful for you to become more aware of how limited you are in your present state of consciousness. Next, spend time contemplating the true meaning of freedom, and what it means to you personally. Decide what it is you want in your life and how you would like to see it unfold. What are your dreams? What would you like to manifest or become during your present incarnation? What are the goals you want to manifest?

Do you realize that you can have it all when you raise your consciousness above your limited perceptions? This is how we have created such a paradise and a life of perfection in Telos. We opened our hearts and minds to perceive and receive the perfection and limitlessness that were the intended way of life on this planet.

It was this way for three long golden ages on this planet, millions of years ago before the fall in consciousness. The fall of mankind is not about Eve eating an apple like some of you still believe. This is an allegory or metaphor and not a very good one either. The fall was about a compromise between the high level of consciousness of those days and a desire to experience polarity. Thus you began to create experiences of doubt and fear, leading to a perception of separation from the perfection that existed.

You consciously gave up the knowledge of higher consciousness and gradually began your descent into the rift of duality that you now experience. Your former knowledge has been lost to your outer awareness for hundreds of thousands of years, and for some, even longer.

This means, beloved ones, that you still possess this knowledge in the deep recesses of your soul and subconscious mind and that you can resurrect it into your present awareness. As you let go of the erroneous and distorted beliefs that have limited you for so long, you will be able to remember your former state and manifest it in your present physical life.

How will it affect my present life?

As you begin to raise your consciousness, your desires, interests and priorities will change. You will begin to realize that you, and only you, are the creator and the prime authority for your life, in spite of all other external appearances. You will gradually take charge of your life, like a master does, instead of being tossed about haphazardly by your external experiences. You will use your new awareness, and the knowledge you gain by the expansion of your consciousness to create a new reality for yourself, the one you always wanted, without limitation.

You will create a life filled with more beauty, more joy, more ease, flow, love and happiness than you could ever have thought possible. This is how raising your consciousness will affect your present life. Gradually, as you begin to open your hearts more to the possibility of this new reality, as you start clearing your emotional and mental bodies of old belief systems that no longer serve you and keep you in your present limitations, all your desires and dreams will manifest in your reality. You will be free to live the kind of life you always wanted, regardless of what it is you desire to create.

What could be the results of raising my consciousness?

The results are infinite and unlimited. In your cosmic evolution, you will continue to raise your consciousness forever, unto eternity. You will recognize your real identity as an eternal and immortal being, a child of Love created by Love. You will know that from Love you came and to greater and greater Love shall you ever expand into. You are the child of a most omniscient and glorious God and are created with all the same attributes, a duplicate, if you will, and nothing less. Your lost memory will be restored.

Even if there are rocks or boulders to remove along the way, thorns to love back to smoothness or steep climbs to master at the beginning of your journey, don't you want to leave behind your limitations and explore the wonders available to you on your planet? This search for Truth can lead to a life of great delight, ease and fulfillment beyond even your wildest dreams and imaginings.

Ask yourself, are you an isolated civilization living on a planet or are we all brothers and sisters, born out of the

Love of the same Creator? Are you alone or are you part of a vast and infinite creation with limitless diversity? As you emerge out of the little box you have been living in, you will discover the "real world." You will realize that your little box has been an illusion and that you are not separate or alone. You are part of All That Is, of Love without end.

What does it mean to ride the wave of Ascension?

You are destined to raise your consciousness from glory to greater and greater glories unto eternity. Most people on the surface are dreaming of going to heaven when they die. Now, with the new cycle unfolding on this planet, you will no longer have to die to go to heaven. Heaven will soon manifest right here on Earth for all those who choose to ride the wave of ascension. Won't you start your most awesome journey now? Or do you choose to retain the consciousness of human struggle? Once you have deeply explored these questions, begin or continue your sacred journey.

Open your heart and consciousness to the other kingdoms of the Earth. You will discover how magical and harmonious they are. Seek to understand who the animals really are, what their role is on this planet and how they can help you. Aside from categorizing them by species, appearance, size and breed, humans on this planet know or understand very little about animals. Open your heart and perception to what is above, below and all around you in the visible and invisible worlds that you have not observed before. As you do this, you will start to open yourself to unconditional love and so much wonderment. You will be raising your consciousness on the waves of ascension energies that are now flooding this planet.

Your ascension to Freedom, your crowning graduation from the thousands of lifetimes spent on this planet, laboring and evolving, is now at hand. Never before in Earth's history has ascension been as easy as it is now, offered to you through the ascension cycle of your Earth Mother. Won't you ride the wave of ascension with Her? Your ascension to your spiritual freedom has been the goal of all your incarnations since the beginning of time. It is the goal of all of the many lifetimes, lessons and wisdom that you have gained while on Earth.

The possibility of ascension to Freedom and Divine Grace can be attained in a few short years. Will you avail yourself of this opportunity now or will you wait another 25,000 years for the next round of ascension on another planet, experiencing the same difficulties you have been subjected to for so long? The choice is yours, dear ones. With Love and Compassion, I am sending you this wake-up call.

Chapter Twelve

Come Home, Beloved Ones, Come Home!
The Fifth Dimension is Awaiting Your Return!

Greetings, this is Adama. With the help and assistance of other very advanced civilizations living deeper within the Earth, our Telosian civilization moved into a fifth dimensional consciousness some time ago. Indeed, we have chosen to remain in a body that has retained a certain level of physical density. Although our bodies are genetically the same as yours, retaining a physical, tangible body that you will be able to see and touch is part of our mission and our agreement to assist the Earth's ascension process.

In our service to life and to this planet, we have agreed that some day, when the surface population is ready to receive us, along with our teachings, this level of physicality will be needed for us to emerge to the surface and be among you as friends, brothers and sisters. Genetically we are the same and the level of physical development and limitlessness we have evolved into will serve as role models for you to consider and embrace for your own development.

Our present DNA code functions with the 12 strands you know about fully activated, and another 24 strands you are just beginning to discover. Most of you have two active strands of DNA and ten that are dormant due to the genetic manipulation that has taken place. With that temporary shielding of so much of your divine potential, you are now functioning with about 5 to 10% of your total potential. We function at 100% of that potential. This potential also expands constantly unto eternity for everyone as they evolve into the higher dimensions.

> *During the time of Lemuria, most of humanity and all Lemurians were functioning with a full 36 strands of DNA.*

During the fall, which was a gradual descent in consciousness that took place over thousands of years, an ongoing dimming of 24 strands of DNA took place, leaving only 12 active ones.

With the sinking of both continents of Lemuria and Atlantis, 10 more strands of DNA became inactive. At this time, all your former faculties can be gradually reactivated as you open yourself to the vibration of unconditional love and higher consciousness. There is much speculation that humanity's genetic coding has been manipulated by extraterrestrials with a desire for control. This is true to some extent for some civilizations on Earth, but know that this was also the karma of humanity at the time. This manipulation occurred with the consent of higher levels of the administrative hierarchy for the Earth.

Human beings had fallen by then to such a low level of consciousness, that it would have been impossible for them to function with all 12 strands of DNA. The consequences of this diminution have been severe and painful. Without humanity's fallen state of consciousness, this alteration of the DNA could not have happened. The shielding of your DNA, "the veil" as it is called, has allowed you to work through your evolution once again from a different viewpoint, without the ability to misuse your powers as happened in the time of Atlantis and Lemuria. It has allowed you to use your free will fully, free of the consequences of the great abuse of power that occurred. You have gained lasting wisdom from your experiences.

In the "Inner Heart," the threefold flame of life of divine Love, divine Wisdom and divine Power used to expand nine feet in diameter within your auric field, and allowed you to function with the god-given faculties that were your divine birthright. You were able to live lifetimes that commonly lasted 20,000 to 30,000 years; the choice was yours. You could live as long as you wanted and leave your incarnation whenever you chose, at will. This threefold flame allowed you a natural immortality, so to speak, and the natural use of the magic and many attributes of your divinity.

You are "immortal gods," created in the image of your Creator, with no limitation. In your distant past, this is how you experienced life on Earth for hundreds of thousands of years. Nothing was withheld from you as divine beings. All knowledge from the universal mind was at your fingertips as your natural birthright. As a collective civilization, you have greatly misused these privileges.

As humanity began to abuse these divine gifts, they gradually diminished. These gifts, my friends, can be regained and maintained only when the original level of consciousness, of unconditional love, harmony, right use of will, right use of power and divine wisdom are maintained in one's awareness, feelings and actions.

At the time of the sinking of both major continents, and the loss of most of the civilizations of Lemuria and Atlantis, it was decreed by Father/Mother God that the only way to return humanity to wholeness and original God-consciousness was to reduce this threefold flame of life to a mere one-sixteenth of an inch. Humanity could no longer misuse God's powers and energies. Ever since, dear ones, you have been functioning with only two strands of DNA and a minute portion of the original threefold flame of life that beats in your heart.

> **Your way back to wholeness has been a**
> **long and painful journey. Know that it**
> **was the only way for God to save you.**

All other attempts your Creator made to bring you back to wholeness failed, and your free will to misuse God's energies was fully honored. There is now a huge silver lining on the horizon. A large percentage of humanity has gained the wisdom and knowledge of its exploration of separation. You have now demonstrated, in the context of free will, your desire to return to wholeness. Your Creator has been waiting for your return with great love and anticipation for the day He could restore all your original gifts back to you.

Your time of redemption is now at hand and all that you have seemingly lost will be fully restored to you. It was never really lost. Your divinity can never be taken away from you, as it is your true nature. It was only veiled in order to allow you to create the lessons, experiences and the knowledge of the divine for all. You left home only to begin your journey back, and now you stand at the threshold of a grand and glorious reunion with all that you are.

> **In Telos, we seem to be so different from you because**
> **we naturally express our full divinity at all times.**

Because of the way we chose to evolve, all the attributes of our divinity were restored a long time ago. The restoration of your divinity will quickly bring you back to the level of grace we now enjoy in our own evolution. We have chosen to remain here in our present state awaiting the day we will merge with the surface dimension and become the role models you need. This mentoring will assist you to quickly embrace the fullness of your God Presence and to manifest it in your daily life. You will know then that we are all the same.

We are your elder brothers and sisters and we love you so very much. How great is our longing to be with you again, face to face, and to assist all of you to come "all the way home." Take our hands and we will not fail you. All the beings of the Light Realm are at your beck and call, making themselves available to assist you in your "homecoming." Come home, my beloveds, come home! The fifth dimension is now awaiting your return.

**We cannot take you home in spite of yourself;
you have to open your heart and mind and
choose daily to return home.**

Those of you who will make this choice will take your physical body "home" with you. At this time of Earth's history, when all life is in the process of redemption, you do not have to leave your body behind as you have for the past several thousand years. You no longer have to physically die. Your body will transform and become immortal and limitless like ours. Consciously choose it, open yourself to it and accept this divine grace from your Heavenly Father/Mother God.

**Will the third dimension still be in
existence after the Great Shift?**

This is a question we cannot fully answer yet with the accuracy you desire. Much is still hanging in the balance, undecided or unknown. It is certain that the third dimension will continue to exist for some time to come, but I can tell you my friends, that for a long time after the Earth shifts, the physical planet will continue to rebalance Herself and it will not be so desirable to be in this dimension.

This is why we encourage you to come along with the Great Shift into the higher dimensions. On this planet several potential timelines exist simultaneously. Each person will experience different scenarios along the timeline they resonate with. Some will choose to stay in the third dimension

115

and these lives may be quite difficult. This is not what we envision or wish for humanity. However, you have free will and your free will is honored to the end.

What is desired for the Earth and by the Earth Mother for Her third dimensional body is to eventually see the third dimension completely healed of all negativity and raised to the highest level possible for that dimension, instead of the low level that has existed for quite some time. She would like to see her body totally restored and expressing the divine perfection and exquisite beauty and balance she knew at the beginning of Her creation.

Though new evolution will no longer take place in the third dimension on this planet after the great shift, the Earth would like to keep alive the opportunity for beings of many kingdoms and civilizations from higher dimensions to continue to enjoy the high degree of physicality in the third dimension whenever they wish.

This can be practiced by humanity, angels and masters as it was on the planet before "the fall," through an easy and conscious lowering of the vibration. They enjoyed the third dimension for as long as they wanted, on vacation as it were, and then returned at will to the higher dimensions. Additionally, once the negativity is eliminated and the Earth restored to Her original state, all beings from all dimensions of this planet and beyond will be able to come here to experience the most lavish and outstanding "vacation resort" the Universe has to offer.

This is the tentative plan, dear ones, but it is not yet guaranteed. Unless you stop trashing and polluting the Earth and raping Her resources now, it may be too late for that restoration.

It can only happen if all of you incarnated right now take a stand to honor and respect the Earth, the Cosmic Mother, who has sustained you with Her love and Her bounty. Her body has provided you with a unique platform for evolution not experienced anywhere else in this universe.

All of you on this planet must take a major stand NOW for Her preservation and restoration. So much of the surface soil and waters have been greatly polluted, devastated, destroyed and depleted, that your planet has reached the point of "no return." You are "the ones" who will decide the future course of existence for the third dimension of our planet. Many of you have chosen to incarnate at this time for the very purpose of assisting the Earth.

Unless you change your destructive ways of treating your "Mother" soon, She will no longer be able to sustain life as you expect Her to. We repeat what we have said before: "Your Mother is a conscious, living, breathing Being of outstanding cosmic magnitude. At this point, She can no longer take abuse from humanity and allow Her third dimensional body to continue to serve you."

When you say that Lemuria still exists today in the higher dimension, where do people continue to live? Does the Inca society still exist in the fifth dimension?

At the time of the sinking of our continent, our Father/Mother God lifted our beloved Lemuria to the level of the fourth dimension where we continued to thrive and evolve. Later on, as we returned to higher ways of life and consciousness, we were restored to the fifth dimensional frequency. Only the third dimensional aspect of Lemuria was destroyed.

You must realize that since we exist in all dimensions simultaneously, Lemuria and the other continents and civilizations existed then in the fourth and fifth dimensions. In the time of Lemuria, before the fall in consciousness, you all consciously traveled those dimensions at will. You could move your vibration between third and fifth dimensions through intention, with great ease and grace, according to what you wanted to do and where you wanted to be.

In those days, all of life thrived in perfect harmony at all times and there were not the veils existing between the dimensions as they do today. These veils were created by the misuse of divine gifts by humanity; paradoxically, this very misuse taught us the greatest wisdom of all. The veils exist as protection for the other dimensions which desire to remain free of the current physical, emotional and spiritual toxicity of the third dimension.

When we say Lemuria was lifted up to the fourth and fifth dimensions, it is with the understanding that Lemuria existed in those dimensions already. What was lifted was the energies and etheric blueprint of the land, of the temples that were still in the service of the Light, and of the people who had remained in alignment with God's plan. It was a lifting up of all the Lemurian energies and culture that had retained a high level of consciousness. All that was still left of Light and Love in the Lemuria of the third dimension at the time of the sinking of the continent, all that could be redeemed to a higher level, was lifted up. It was a joining and a merging of the energies of the remnant of the third dimension with the fourth.

The Inca civilization ascended quite some time ago to the fifth dimension where it is continuing its evolution and the people are waiting to welcome you into their midst.

Will Lemuria simply reappear in the Pacific Ocean? Will the topography of the Earth be totally different?

It is not likely that the whole continent of Lemuria will reappear in the Pacific Ocean in the third dimension. At best, several of the islands in the Pacific that were once mountaintops in the time of Lemuria will get larger with much more land around them. The topography of the Earth will undergo some great changes as it shifts to a higher level of consciousness, but it will not be considered totally different.

The Earth is about to undergo some major changes. Your Earth Mother needs to cleanse and revitalize herself before she is lifted up to the fifth dimension. We ask you to allow Her these changes without judgment. She has tolerated much abuse from humanity upon Her body for millions of years, allowing you your experience of free will. She has received little gratitude and respect in return and no longer has any choice but to renew herself if she is going to continue hosting an evolving humanity at a higher level. Consider all that is to happen a "healing crisis," a necessary step in the purification of Earth's physical and etheric bodies.

In return, we ask you now to show compassion and to allow and support Her cleansing and renewal. It will be for your benefit as well, even if there may be the appearance of chaotic circumstances for a while. Life on this planet, as you know it, is about to experience a series of major transformations.

The bell is ringing for the completion of an era that has been difficult and painful for humanity.

After the changes, you will be able to retain a certain level of physicality as we do. You will be able to experience yourself as "real" and physical, just as you are now. Your very being, and everything around you, will have shifted to a new level of perfection, expansion and clarity. You will be integrating a new level of consciousness and perfection. As you change your perception, everything around you will adjust and change with it.

The Earth, along with a major portion of humanity, is now embarking upon a great adventure. You have prayed for divine intervention in your world, and your prayers are about to be answered. First, you must clean up the mess you have and still are creating in the third dimension, and allow your Earth Mother to cleanse her body. You must acknowledge that the Earth is your cosmic Mother that has provided your platform for evolution.

Be aware that the Earth's resources that you consume so lavishly and take for granted, cause great depletion upon and within her body. Do you realize that the trees you cut so freely and in such large numbers are her lungs, that her crystals represent her artery system, and that her oil you so relentlessly and extravagantly burn is her very blood? Her minerals and gems that you mine without any consideration are part of her energy system. You must learn to use the resources of the Earth in a much more conscious and respectful manner than you have up to now.

You must also begin to perceive the consciousness of higher dimensions in order to be admitted there.

Hold Peace and Love in Your Hearts

Galatia of Telos

Greetings dear ones, my name is Galatia, the one known as Adama's wife in Telos.

I am delighted to be here on this beautiful day in the midst of the sweetness of all of you, as well as the sweetness of the Earth, to share my love and my peace with you. Truly, our meeting here today is a most sacred occasion, and we know that there will be many more of these gatherings to come.

It is my desire to reinforce within your consciousness the importance of getting the message of Lemuria out to the populace of the Earth at this time.

There are many beings in Lemuria such as myself, Adama, Ahnahmar, Celestia, Angelina, and several others, coming forth at this time to touch the hearts of those who have forgotten their Lemurian roots. It is sad indeed that because it has been too painful for humanity to remember, such an important part of the history of Earth was lost for such a long time.

Now, we join together as brothers and sisters of the past, present and future time of Lemuria and Telos, to awaken your memories of what Lemuria was like. We bring forth to you our treasures, our history, our hearts, and our memories to ignite and instill the heart-felt remembrance for those who were there, as well as for those who were not there.

To those whose hearts yearn for the wisdom of a civilization of light, love, nurturing and unity, we now gradually unveil our history to your outer consciousness. Into the present from the past, through voices such as yours, we ask to assist those on the Earth plane in creating and birthing the New Earth.

For many years, dearest ones, you have prayed for heaven on earth, not really knowing what you were praying for or how it could manifest in your world. You all know that for a very long time, life has not been so easy on the surface. Many times your lives have felt more like a journey through hell rather than one through heaven. And "Heaven on earth" were words spoken only in prayers, or cherished in fleeting thoughts of what life could be like without the knowingness of your true heart. It is not enough to just remember patterns through words; it is much more important to remember patterns through the energies of the heart.

Your group joining together today, with the intention of re-awakening the remembrance of the heart of Lemuria, continues to assist the revitalization of these remembrances which once only seemed to be part of a lost history. Yet, these memories have continued to live, to thrive and to survive unto this now moment in time. They are reconnected into the present and can assist in co-creating the new. In Telos, we are honored and excited to assist you. We are excited about the part we can play towards the unification of the vision for the New Earth. It is our supreme honor and delight to work with those who are ready to receive this information and wisdom for the transformation of many.

Today, we send our divine love and blessings to all of you. We tell you that we have long awaited the time of the great reunion with those on the surface. We ask for your receptivity and openness regarding new teachings and concepts that will be presented to you for your personal awakening and planetary evolution. Hold your vision high for the future of your planet and the kind of world you want for yourselves. No matter what else you deem important to your survival at this time, do not hesitate to stop when beckoned by your heart to listen and remember, to love and to feel love.

If you want peace, love and prosperity, beloveds, hold those divine qualities in your heart in perfect harmony and unity of consciousness. What you really want to manifest, you must first unite with consciously in great love. At this pivotal time of Earth's transition, we request that you seriously reconsider your true values and priorities. Be sure that what you consider to be your priorities and deepest values are fulfilling the intentions and goals you had set for yourself prior to your present incarnation.

Remember, beloved ones, that everything you do on the Earth plane is always temporary and part of the passage of time, but whatever you become by embracing your divine nature remains with you for eternity.

Live each moment of each day with the conscious awareness that you are a divine being having a human experience.

Remember that you have chosen to come here at this time, in this incarnation, with the intention and determination to immortalize your body and your incarnation by fully embodying all the qualities of your divinity.

Be fully aware that your divinity will not manifest automatically without your dedicated intention and moment-by-moment conscious participation.

- Whatever you do in all aspects of daily life, always do it as an act of love.

- Whatever you say, always share words of wisdom, love, compassion and understanding.

- Whatever you allow yourself to think in your daily internal dialogue, embrace the consciousness of God and the light realms.

- Soon the paradise you are seeking will be yours to enjoy.

I want to impart to you, in this brief sharing, that you are deeply loved by all of us in Telos. We are always so pleased each time you choose to reconnect with us. On behalf of the Lemurian sisterhood of Telos, I convey our deepest friendship and love to all of you.

All creation begins first
In your imagination.
It is your tool for conscious manifestation.
Use it to create positively,
And your wildest dreams will manifest.
- Adama

Chapter Thirteen

The Great Jade Lemurian Temple of Telos and The Flame of Healing, A Fifth Ray Activity

Adama speaks to us about healing and Lemuria. A profound meditation takes us to the Great Jade Temple of Telos, where what we experience is incredibly healing and refreshing.

Greetings, my friends, this is Adama of Telos. Whenever we are invited to share our teachings, it is always a time of great joy and fulfillment for us in Telos. Today, we would like to discuss a new approach to healing and introduce you to a wonderful healing temple we have in Telos, called the Great Jade Temple. Access to this awesome temple has been closed to surface dwellers since the sinking of our continent 12,000 years ago.

Recently, however, the doors of this great temple of healing have been re-opened to all who wish to visit. You are invited to come here in your etheric bodies to recharge, purify and learn to heal with a new level of understanding. This new dispensation is indeed a privilege that all of you on the surface can take advantage of during this monumental time of change and healing for humanity and for the planet.

The Great Jade Temple was physical in the time of Lemuria, and its main focus has always been healing in the true sense

125

of the word. Since its construction hundreds of thousands of years ago, its energies have blessed the lives of the people. Inside the temple has burned the immortal, unfed flame of healing for the planet. This healing flame has been constantly nurtured by the angelic kingdom, by the Holy Spirit and also by the love of the people of Lemuria. The energies of this temple have held the balance of true healing for the planet itself, for her inhabitants and for your Earth Mother as well.

When we realized that our continent was in danger and would eventually be destroyed, we also knew that this great temple would be lost in its physical expression. We therefore decided to build a physical replica in Telos. Although the replica is a bit smaller than the original temple, all the records of the energies of the "Immortal Flame of Healing" since the time of its creation were transferred here to Telos. It is still gathering momentum to this day. This awesome healing energy was never lost to this planet, in spite of the destruction of our continent. All of its energies and treasures were moved prior to Lemuria's demise.

Planning for the building of the replica and moving the energy of the temple took place a couple of thousand years before Lemuria went down. Replicas of many other important temples were also built in Telos at the same time. In order to save our culture and as many of our people as possible, we had to plan our strategy 5,000 years ahead of the actual time of the foreseen cataclysms.

Healing is so greatly needed at this time for all of you, and this is why we have opened the doors of the Great Jade Temple to assist humanity now.

It is our great pleasure to invite you to come here in your etheric body at night to receive a much greater understanding of true healing. When you come here, we have as guides a great number of our people who are always willing to take you "under their wings" spiritually to assist you in healing the deep traumas and sorrows of the past and present. As you heal your inner pain and traumas, you will also heal the difficult conditions in your lives and your physical bodies.

External pains and difficulties are always the mirrors of inner pains and fears. They mirror to you what needs to be healed and transformed in your consciousness. We can assign three counselors for each of you who come here; they can assist you with whatever is most needed for your return to wholeness. One counselor focuses with you on your emotional body, another focuses with you on your mental body and a third one focuses on the healing of your physical body, all in total harmony and synchronicity. In this way, your healing becomes more balanced than if you just focus on one aspect of yourself, without understanding and transforming your internal programming. Understand that when one aspect of yourself is not in perfect balance, it affects all other aspects of your being.

How does one get to the Great Jade Temple in his or her etheric body?

Through intention, my friend! What you need to do is to set your intention to come to this temple in your meditation or before you go to sleep at night. As an example, you may say the following prayer to your God Self and your guides and masters: *"From the Lord God of my Being, I request to be taken to the Great Jade Temple in Telos tonight. I now ask my guides, masters and angels to take me there as my body rests from the activities of the day."* You may also formulate your own prayer requests. Set the intention that you want to come here for recharging, for purification, for healing, for counseling, or simply to have communion and interaction with us under the energies of the flame of healing.

We know how to take care of you once you get here. Basically, in your higher soul body you know how to get here yourself; simply trust that it is happening, even if you do not have any conscious recollection of your experience when you wake up. Your etheric body looks almost identical to your physical body except it is more perfected. It also feels as physical to you when you are here. In the future, your transformed body will also feel very physical to you, although it will be relieved of much density and the frequency will vibrate at a much higher rate.

In the process of transforming your consciousness and your physical body, you are not losing anything. You are integrating higher, more subtle vibrations and greater light. All you will be losing is much unwanted density. Your body will become much more refined, much more beautiful, limitless, immortal and will feel just as physical as it does now. You will not experience limitation of any kind; the veils will be removed. You will travel at the speed of Light. It is going to be a lot of fun, I promise!

What would be an appropriate request for one to bring to the temple for healing?

Basically on this planet most people have physical problems of some sort, and many hidden fears which create challenges in your daily life. You have emotions trapped in your subconscious and unconscious mind that were imprinted on your soul from many past experiences that were not only painful, but often very traumatic. These experiences were the lessons that were learned along your evolutionary pathway. Everyone has an accumulation of emotional trauma in their feeling body from many thousands of embodiments. Resolution is now needed for final clearing, healing and for the integration of the greater wisdom for which these experiences were created. Any experience that was not cleared in a given lifetime keeps replaying the same programming again and again in all subsequent lifetimes until true healing, wisdom and understanding take place in the depth of the soul.

The sadness, sorrow, grief, emotional trauma, and anything you experience that does not reflect the natural joy, bliss and ecstasy of your being indicate what needs healing within yourself. Conscious and subconscious fears hold everyone back and need to be cleared. Mental toxins coming from lifetimes of embracing erroneous belief systems and distorted programming are now surfacing in one way or another to be finally cleared and healed. Pay attention to the promptings of your soul and bring to the temple at night those pressing issues so much in need of healing and resolution.

Our guides will discuss with you the lessons and wisdom you need to understand and what steps you can take to achieve true and permanent healing. Your healing can be compared to the peeling of a huge onion with hundreds of layers. You heal one layer at a time until completion. You then become a perfect mirror of your divinity and all things open to you, beyond your wildest dreams.

Much of this work, but not all, can be done at night while your body sleeps and can later be integrated in your daily life. You don't need to know what every fear and all past experiences are about. All you need to do is consciously release these energies, whatever they are called, and however they are felt, as they come up in your consciousness. This is the kind of work our counselors can do with you as they have access to your akashic records. They can give you much insight for your healing. In turn, you bring back and integrate this new wisdom within your subconscious, and in your waking state, you can begin to apply it. Your meditations with your Divine Presence will resurrect a greater awareness of who you truly are. If you wish to ascend within the next decade, clearing and healing yourself must become your main priority.

129

***Your inner work is the most important task
for you at this time to accelerate your evolution and to prepare for your homecoming.***

Our counselors at the temple will give you, at the soul level,
a broadened perspective of why you are experiencing certain
health problems. They will show you why certain difficulties
persist in your life and how you have created them, be they
physical, mental or emotional. With the assistance of our
counselors, you will learn to heal yourself and all the pain
and distortions imprinted in your soul. Before any complete
and permanent physical healing can take place, the emotional causes or distortions in your belief system have to be
addressed and released. I'm not referring to band-aid solutions, but to permanent healing.

Know that all physical problems, even if they appear to be
accidents, are always rooted in the emotional and mental
bodies. Mental stress and mental illnesses also have their
roots in the emotions. The emotional body is the starting
point for permanent healing. The traumas suffered during the destruction of Lemuria and Atlantis, when people
were separated from loved ones and families overnight, gave
birth to much fear, sadness, sorrow and despair in the souls
of humanity, and you have carried these traumas forward
lifetime after lifetime.

It is now time to completely heal the past and embrace a
brand new paradigm of love, personal empowerment and
unprecedented grace for your life and for the planet. In
Telos, we are your brothers and sisters, close friends of the
past who love you all so very much. It is our joy to extend
to you all the assistance we are allowed at this time to complete your transformation, resurrection and ascension into
the realms of Love and Light.

We are aware that the level of pain on the surface has been
so great that many of you have closed your hearts as a

means of protection from the pain you could no longer endure. You have chosen to live in the survival mode instead of embracing the joy of living.

We have also disconnected from so many wondrous aspects of ourselves in order to survive here in this third dimension. How can we heal this trauma now in a few short years and prepare for the great planetary shift?

You can accomplish this through a deep surrender to the inner process of healing. The "I AM" of your being knows exactly how to assist you in your total healing and take you all the way back home in the least painful manner. Healing the pain of the past is a gradual process but also the greatest adventure of all your many incarnations here, and the one that will open the doors of your soul to your spiritual freedom. It is leading you, step by step, to reconnect consciously with all the wondrous aspects of your Greater Self. In the process, your hearts will open a thousandfold. As your hearts open, you will begin to see and understand all that has happened through the eyes of the soul.

Your heart is the great intelligence of your soul and is one with the mind of God. It knows everything, holds all memories of all aspects of you since the beginning, and it will never mislead you. Your heart is the part of your beingness that you must learn to know and really trust again. You have closed your hearts, dear ones, because your pain and fear have been so great. Closure was a form of protection for you in the past. It served your evolution in wondrous ways that you will come to understand one day, but now it no longer serves you. It is time for all of you to finally come "home" to the Light and Love of your divinity.

Many of you still cling to your old pain and fears simply because you are afraid to open your hearts to unconditional love and release your erroneous beliefs. You fear that if you open your hearts to life unconditionally, you may suffer even more pain. Old fears and pain have become so familiar to you that you have found a distorted level of security and comfort in them.

How do we actually open our hearts and allow our emotional bodies to begin the healing process?

There is no recipe that will work for everyone. Each one is unique and has different issues to heal. Each one of you has a different emotional make-up and your own distinct healing process, but success for all will be achieved. Basically, you start the process through choice, sustained intention, and conscious and active meditation. Daily communication with your higher self is also essential. Ask that part of you that remains in divine wholeness to reveal what needs healing in the now moment, and to bring it forth into your conscious awareness.

Start signaling to your I AM Presence with serious intention that you want to ascend and be whole again, and that you want to reconnect and integrate all parts of yourself. Willingly surrender your desire with trust and love to whatever process is necessary to receive that healing. Be assured that you will receive the full cooperation of your higher self and the whole of the light realm. Your healing will take place at every level.

Your higher self has been waiting for your return to grace for a very long time. Be assured of its full cooperation. Never allow yourself to judge the process. Soon, you will find yourself on the other side, in this wondrous world you have been longing and dreaming about through the ages. Your higher self communicates with you through your emotions. This means that you need to pay attention to what you are feeling at all times. If it is not pleasant, simply release it through the fires of the heart and keep moving to the next healing, and the next, until you are whole again.

Your higher self will draw to you the right books, the right people and the right opportunities to ensure your success. If you open your mind and heart to your healing with sustained intention and diligence, the process can unfold with ease and grace.

Your healing process will continue to progress as you remain focused in your intention. It may appear to be a lot of work at first, and without doubt, it is. See it as a journey back to the "sun" of your being and know that the process is filled with rewards and fulfillment along the way. You are not alone in this journey. All your angels, guides, masters, as well as all of us in the New Lemuria, are accompanying you at every step. The entire spiritual hierarchy of this planet, your Earth Mother and the whole of the light realm are at your beck and call to assist your healing. Know that you deserve our love and assistance. Never hesitate to ask.

As your healing progresses, your energy will come back. Your physical body will start letting go of the pain and traumas of the past and you will begin to rejuvenate. You will feel yourself becoming more alive and vibrant. Humanity has been working with 5% to 10% of its full potential as divine beings. The rest of your being has been there all along in a state of slumber. Wake-up and heal yourselves. As you open your hearts and let go of your pain, you will become more and more alive. The joy you feel will be amplified many times. Your mental faculties will expand and you may discover a new sense of awe and freedom. Consciously open yourself to grace and allow yourself to receive those energies in your body daily.

Do we actually ever reach a point where the healing is done?

Yes, my friend. Every time you work these things out within yourself, you go deeper and deeper. You are peeling off layers, and some of them go very deep. When you think you have reached the last layer, you start feeling better and you think the healing is complete; but then, the pain may surface again to be healed on a much deeper level. This is why now, in this particular time of the last incarnation for many of you, the healing process seems more endless than ever before. In this lifetime, everything comes together, not from one or two or six incarnations, but from the totality of your incarnations on the Earth. Most of you have had thousands of incarnations on this planet. Everything manifests now in your lives to be healed, every little thing. It may appear worse now than before because you are consciously looking at it.

Does the toxicity we encounter in our daily lives impact the speed of our healing process?

Well yes, it adds to your burdens. Let me explain this. You have various bodies, what you call subtle bodies You also have four main body systems; the physical vehicle, the emotional body, the mental body and the etheric body. Each of these has a number of sublevels as well; that is why we talk of 9 subtle bodies or 12 subtle bodies or more. We will not explore all of this now as it is too complex for this discussion. We will focus on the main four bodies that each represent 25% of your totality. They work together, so when you suppress one you suppress the others. When you heal one, you bring relief to the others. It is important to know that when you ingest or inhale toxic chemical substances, certain of them are fairly easy to clear from the body, while with others the body has no mechanism of elimination.

Twenty-first century chemicals and pollution have been so thoroughly incorporated into your food, water, and air supply, the body has great difficulty eliminating them. The levels of toxins within your bodies continues to build. When the body was designed, these man-made toxic substances did not exist. They have a tendency to lodge in the cells, and only the right application of homeopathic and vibrational remedies can eliminate those undesirable vibrations. It is quite complicated. Do what you can to ingest into your bodies only the purest type of water and foods. When you do not feel well physically, your emotions rise up and your mental faculties are not as sharp. When you do not feel emotionally balanced, your physical body doesn't feel well either because it is all connected. When your thoughts are negative or in judgment, you lower the vibration of all your bodies. You cannot separate any part of yourself without affecting the whole.

> **What I am becoming aware of is the realization that we can never be whole until we awaken, and until we heal each one of these bodies.**

You cannot become whole if you avoid healing any part of your energetic make-up. True and permanent healing takes place when you create balanced healing at all levels. There are people who are physically ill, let's say with cancer. They spend a fortune in trying to achieve physical healing by the cut, burn and poison modalities of the medical establishment but their emotional state, which may in part have caused the cancer, is never addressed. In fact, these treatments add much more stress and trauma to the already overburdened emotional body. What kind of permanent healing can be expected from such denial of a basic aspect of Self?

Billions of dollars are being spent each year in the application of band-aid solutions. Some people experience temporary remission at times, but what occurs is not true and permanent healing. Even if temporary or short-term relief is gained, if the soul has not gained any understanding or wisdom from experiencing the illness, true healing has not taken place. If the person dies from the cut, burn and poison method, healing and understanding are not achieved because the root of the problems in the emotional body were ignored. Whatever the cause of the cancer, if not addressed in one lifetime, will be repeated again in subsequent incarnations until the deeper understanding and wisdom are learned.

Your I AM Presence requires that you learn all of your lessons of wisdom and truth before you can access your total spiritual freedom and your return to wholeness. This is why you have had so many incarnations.

Angels and many other beings from the light realm working with humanity come regularly to the temple for purification and recharging. The Great Jade Temple serves as a means of decontamination for them, a setting in which to unload the discordant energies picked up from their contact with surface humanity.

Your God Self works from the level of creation. It works very closely with angels, ascended masters and with us in facilitating your healing. We are never permitted to perform healings for you without the permission of your Divine Presence. In all your efforts to heal yourself, you must include and reconnect with your I AM Presence and state your intention for whatever it is you want to accomplish or heal. If we did it for you, how could you ever become a master of divine expression?

Sometimes, people get angry with the ascended masters or angelic presences because they feel their prayer requests have not been answered the way they expected. In doing so, they deny the divine source of their desires, closing their hearts to further assistance.

Perhaps you asked a certain ascended master to receive the money to go on a trip, and the trip did not materialize. Or you wanted to manifest a relationship with a specific person, and it did not happen either. Instead of surrendering the issue to divine grace and the greater wisdom of your Divinity, who knows what is best for your chosen pathway for this life, you become angry at God or the ascended master. You decide you will no longer have anything to do with them, and you close the door.

This kind of attitude, beloved ones, is common in humanity. Those engaging in such emotions deprive themselves of much assistance, grace and blessings for that given incarnation. What you don't realize is that no ascended master or angelic presence can go beyond the pathway of your soul. Your "I AM" knows exactly what you need to learn and accomplish to meet the goals you set for this lifetime. Any angel or ascended master will always work in full cooperation with your Divine Self to assist your "greater plan" and ultimate destiny. While you are in the third dimension, you are veiled and do not see the broader perspective of your incarnation.

Your "I AM" is your governor, and your soul represents the sum total of all your experiences. Ascension is the process of unifying all of this into oneness; you become totally whole again. You become the personification of your Divine Self, manifesting the fullness of your divinity. The final stage of ascension is the most wonderful event that could ever happen in anyone's evolution. For so many lifetimes you have worked toward that one goal, and in this lifetime you can achieve it fully. You can become all that you ever wanted to be, because the doors of ascension are now wide open, like never before in millions of years.

This is your chance to say yes to this great opportunity. All the help and assistance you need will be provided. Be wise and take advantage of this rare window of opportunity. Ascension doors close and open, according to various cycles of evolution. It may be a long time before they open as wide again. I would say to all of you, if you want to gain your spiritual freedom in this lifetime, to become totally unlimited and to experience the alchemical marriage of your soul with your God Self through the process of the ascension, there is no better time than now to achieve it. You must consciously and intentionally choose it and want it more than anything else. You are not going to be forced into it.

You are being offered at this time the greatest of all opportunities. Will you take our hands and accept our assistance for your homecoming? We are already home. Will you come and join us?

Conscious Meditation to the Great Jade Temple

The Great Jade Temple is a famous and sacred place where beings from all dimensions on this planet and beyond come for healing. Those of the light realms who directly assist humanity also come to this temple to cleanse and recharge their energies. It is used by galactic beings as well. This healing temple is visited by many civilizations. It is mainly constructed of the purest concentration of jade.

I ask now that you center yourself in your heart; sit comfortably and relax; begin to receive and integrate the healing energies. You are now invited to come with me on a journey in consciousness to Telos to experience the Great Jade Temple beneath Mount Shasta. You are traveling here in your etheric body. As you continue to focus in your heart, ask your higher self and your guides to take you along for this experience. There are many of us there, waiting to receive you. Invite your guides to take you to Telos in consciousness to the portal of the Great Jade Temple. All your guides are familiar with this place, and they know exactly how to take you there.

Totally relax your body and breathe deeply as you focus your intention to visit the Great Jade Temple. Now imagine yourself there. See yourself arriving at the portal of this huge temple, a four-sided pyramid made of the finest quality of jade stones. The head priest, a guardian of this temple, greets you. Notice the floor tiled with jade and pure gold. Fountains of golden green luminescent light are shooting their essence about 30 feet in the air from several areas, creating a very mystical effect. Feel yourself there and look at whatever is shown to you. Feel the air that you are now breathing in the temple and feel the invigorating energy created by all the fountains of pure healing energy permeating the air everywhere. How refreshing and rejuvenating it is for your whole body! Though you are there in your etheric body, you will bring back some of this vibration to your physical body when you return. That is why it is so important to breathe in deeply, taking in as much of the healing energy as you can.

Flowers of all shapes, sizes and colors, along with a large variety of emerald green plants, are growing in large jade boxes creating a most magical environment. As you gaze upon this most magical beauty, feel the energies of the temple. Keep taking in as much of this energy as you can.

The Head Priest introduces each one of you to a member of our community of Telos who will be your guide and assistant for your journey here. As you enter the temple with your guide, you see a very large stone made of pure jade, oval shaped, about 10 feet in diameter and 6 feet high. This stone resonates with the purest and highest healing vibration. On the top of the stone, you see a round chalice made of gold and jade. It has a flat base and sides about ten inches high. It is hosting the emerald green unfed Flame of Healing that has been burning to assist humanity for millions of years.

Now feel this huge flame deeply in your soul, in your heart and in your emotional body. Yes, you can also take your emotional body there. This awesome flame burns perpetually and maintains a major healing energy matrix for the planet. This flame has consciousness, my friends. It is fed eternally by the love of the Holy Spirit, the angelic kingdom and our love as well. As you approach the Jade stone, you are invited by the Guardian of the Healing Flame to sit on a chair made of pure jade, and to meditate and contemplate what in your life needs healing the most. What changes in your consciousness are you willing to make to bring about that healing?

While in meditation, you are receiving telepathic guidance and assistance from your guides and this guidance is imprinted in your heart and soul. Now, we will pause for you to have this interaction with your guides and with your higher self for your healing. *(Pause)* See and feel the jewels, the crystals and healing energies of the temple and breathe them in. Breathe in this healing energy deeply, as much as you can; you are going to take this energy back into your physical body. Keep breathing it in. You are in one of the most sacred healing sites on this planet. Take as long as you need, there is no hurry.

When you feel complete, get up from your chair and walk around the temple with your guide. Absorb all the beauty and the healing energy you can. Feel free to communicate to him/her the burdens of your heart and ask for further assistance for your healing. Be open to whatever is revealed to you. If you do not remember your journey consciously, do not be concerned. For most of you, it is not yet meant to be and you are getting the information at some other level.

When you feel complete, come back to consciousness in your body and take several deep breaths. Know that you can return there any time you want. Each time you will be assisted in the same manner. The more often you return, the greater the rapport you create with us and the greater momentum you generate for your healing. We are reaching out to you. We ask you now to respond and reach out to us as well. It can only work when we all cooperate together.

We now conclude this meditation by sending you love, peace

and healing. We are holding our hands out to you with love, guidance and assistance. We are only as far away as a thought, a whisper or a request from your heart. And so be it! I am Adama.

Part Three

Messages from Various Beings

When you put yourself
Into a state of total trust,
The universe responds,
And begins providing immediately.
And I mean "total trust,"
Not a cocktail of trust and fear.
- Adama

Chapter Fourteen

Messages from El Morya

The Consciousness that Functions on "Automatic Pilot" is Not Heading for the Ascension Door

Greetings, beloved ones,

I am El Morya, the guardian of the focus of the Will of God for this planet. From our abodes within Mount Shasta, Adama and I wish to bring you a message of Love. Our message is a wake-up call, dear ones, because we know that time is now getting very short for all of you.

Adama has described the state of consciousness or attitude in which so many precious souls of Earth allow themselves to live on "automatic pilot," a state of spiritual slumber. In that state, people do not consciously create their reality nor do they live their lives in accordance with their soul purposes or the goals they chose before coming into this incarnation.

Because we love you so very much, it is our great desire to greet all of you at the portal of the fifth dimension around the year 2012. As we open wide the portal and lay out the golden carpet for your arrival, it will be our delight to bid you welcome to the realms of Light and Love. What a wondrous and joyous day this will be for us and for those of you who step through this Door! What a happy reunion it will be for us all! A great reception is being prepared. There will be the shedding of many tears on that great day, but this time, dear ones, they will be tears of pure joy and ecstasy.

Can you imagine, just for a moment, the joy you will experience when you meet consciously, in your immortalized body, face to face with those you have loved dearly in your present life? You will also meet those whom you may not remember at this time, but who are souls you have been close to and loved just as dearly in other lifetimes. They are the ones you have known for millennia, your eternal friends with whom you have incarnated again and again, as well as other members of your soul family who love you so profoundly.

As we share this information, we already feel the joy and excitement that this wondrous day will bring. Your loved ones are waiting to embrace you with much expectation. They will all be there near "the Door," robed in garments of Light and Glory, waiting to welcome you in their arms as you enter.

As our channel Aurelia Louise receives these words from us, tears are rolling down her cheeks at the thought of rejoining the souls of Light who were her parents in this present life, and with other members of her family who made their transition to the "other side" during her childhood. As she writes and wipes her tears, they are also present with her in spirit, watching and sending their love, looking forward with great anticipation to the day of the Great Reunion. That day will be so wondrous that the whole of Creation will be watching. I repeat myself again; it is the most sincere desire of the spiritual hierarchy of this planet and your Father/Mother God to see all of you make it to this sacred portal and step through.

Beloved ones, out of our great love for you, we of the spiritual hierarchy, wish to remind you once again that there is a "code of entry" into the fifth dimension. There are jokes in your world about "Peter" standing at the gate of heaven and deciding who will or will not be allowed entrance into the Kingdom. Well, my friends, this is not so much of a joke here. There is more truth to this than many of you may realize at this time.

I say this because there is a gate or a portal at which one must qualify for admission. I, El Morya, was embodied as the disciple Peter in the time of Jesus. Now I have become the Chohan and the Guardian of the First Ray of the Will of God for the people of Earth. This means that I am also the guardian of that portal.

The Will of God, dear ones, is the first portal one must enter in order to progress in the right direction on the spiritual path. You must be willing to surrender your human ego and human personality to the Will of God, to be refined and transformed into the Divine, to walk your true spiritual path. Divine Will is the first portal. There are six others you must also qualify for before you can reach the door of the fifth dimension for your planetary ascension.

To go through this first portal, it is highly recommended that you take my classes on the Inner Planes *(while your body sleeps)* or those from my co-workers of the Will of God. You must pass my tests in your waking state before you can move on to the next portal. Many of you reading this have already moved through this first portal in this life or in the past, and some of you have passed through other portals as well. We deplore the fact that a large percentage of humanity is still living their lives on "automatic pilot." They have no idea where they are going, why they are incarnated on Earth, nor do they want to find out. They live their lives from day to day, with no conscious direction, their minds and hearts scattered to the four winds, following the path of least resistance in spiritual slumber.

147

On the threshold of such a monumental event, one that humanity has been waiting and longing for hundreds of thousands of years, there are still too many precious souls who have not presented themselves to the Counsel of Light at the entrance to the portal of which I am in charge. I, and my co-worker Adama, along with several others, are joining together to see if we can give you one more "wake-up" call. If you have not yet made it to the portal of the "Will of God," we want you to know that it is still possible to catch up and pass through the other portals "on time" if you choose to do so.

There is no more time for procrastination. You must awaken now and earnestly apply spiritual laws in all aspects of your life, living by the concepts of Love from day-to-day. Let go of your fears and preconceived ideas about God. Be willing to embrace the Truth that you have cleverly avoided. Become the God that you are, right now, by becoming Love in action in all you think, say and do. Love is the only shortcut you can use in your ascension process. It is the great key, love of Self, love of God and love for all the Earth kingdoms. Love and honor all that breathe the Life of the Creator.

Let go of all judgments and embrace the way of harmlessness. With enough Love in your heart, you can make it through all the portals to the ascension door ... on time. Be assured it will not happen for those who continue to live their lives on "automatic pilot."

All who arrive at the ascension door will have to pass the seven initiations in order to acquire the codes of entry and qualify for planetary ascension. Each one of those seven initiations has seven levels of testing. It used to take several lifetimes of diligent application of the spiritual laws to be able to pass through one or more of those initiations. At this very unique time in Earth history, there is an unprecedented dispensation by which each soul, with serious and diligent application, can accomplish this in a few years. I, El Morya, shall be there, as the "Peter" you are familiar with, along with the rest of the spiritual hierarchy and your loved ones to welcome every one of you "Back Home."

I am your eternal friend, El Morya.

The Christing of Our Planet Has Begun

It is my pleasure and honor to give a transmission for the English-speaking population who will read the Telos information. I want you to know that you are all very dear to my heart. This information is very important and timely, and I would like to suggest that you take it very deeply into your heart and consciousness. It will greatly assist you in opening your awareness and perception of the higher dimensions.

This material gives you an idea of how life was originally meant to be expressed on this planet. It also gives you a glimpse of the direction the Earth is taking for the future of humanity. What is ahead is so wondrous, it simply cannot be described in a book. The whole plan cannot be revealed at this time either. The Telos books give you a very good introduction to the wonders that await you when you open yourself to your higher consciousness and divinity.

It is also important that this information
be shared with all those who are open to it.
This is part of your homework, my friends.

The time has come for the Lemurian consciousness to be revived and known again on the surface of this planet. It represents the consciousness of the "Source Energy of your Creator." It is nothing less than the return of the Christ consciousness in its most practical form for all to apply. The New Lemuria is not just a place to go; it is most of all a state of being, of perfection, of Christhood and divinity manifested in a fifth dimensional vibration, retaining a luminous and perfected level of physicality.

The time you have awaited for so long is just over your shoulders!

All ascended civilizations, on this planet and beyond, are now vigilantly working together in unity and harmony to assist the ascension of Mother Earth and of humanity. This is the time you have waited for so many incarnations. I suggest that you remain centered in your heart and focused within your divine presence through all the changes and the purification of the planet. The "New World" you have hoped for, transformed as you have desired, is now about to manifest. I guarantee you that there is nothing to fear. Your Creator is taking this planet back from the energies of rancor and hate, and the vibration of peace and love will soon be in charge again. All of the Light Realms are offering their assistance for the process of your transformation and transition into the new world. What is taking place at this moment upon your planet is so awesome that this Universe and many others are focused upon you.

What is about to happen has never been done in any system of worlds, solar system or galaxy anywhere.

The transformation that you are about to experience is unique to this planet. You have become, brave ones, the "showcase of this universe." There are millions upon millions of spaceships, with their large crews and passengers, watching you and sending their love and support.

It is most important that you let go of all your attachments to how things have been and how they should be. Let go of all your old belief systems and structures. Life, as you know it at the moment, is about to change drastically for the better. The purification of your planet will open the way for the transformation that is now on its way. It is no longer an event that you anticipate for the future, my friends, "the time is now!"

Those of you who choose to ignore or deny the information given will not be able to do so for very long.

A much more intense level of energy, designed to bring about the Christing of your planet, began to flood the Earth around May 1ˢᵗ of 2002. This energy is now bombarding the Earth, day and night, and will continue to accelerate and intensify until you are comfortably nestled in the bliss of the fifth dimension. If you are not interested in acceleration and change, you will sooner or later leave this incarnation and incarnate somewhere else that is more appropriate. There are other third dimensional planets similar to yours at the present time willing to host your life-stream and allow you to continue your evolution at your own pace. There is no obligation to come along; the choice is entirely yours.

Know that the long cycle of third dimensional life on this planet is coming to an end. Your Earth Mother has now chosen to graduate and to receive the crown of her ascension. This means that very soon, she will host on her body only an enlightened civilization. There are also those who, for various reasons, will not be ready to ascend in this life, but will qualify in their very next incarnation. They are the souls who will reincarnate here again in the new world to complete their evolution and make their ascension the next time. These beloved souls will become the children of the future generation.

As I mentioned, I am one of the Guardians of the gate of the fifth dimension. Your surrender to the "Divine Will" will bring much ease and grace to your journey. It is my great desire to welcome you there personally when the time comes. I am renewing my invitation for you to come to Mount Shasta in your etheric body at night to attend our nightly classes. The focus of our classes is to prepare your consciousness for the "great shift." The Mount Shasta Brotherhood of Light and the Lemurian Brotherhood of Light, as well as many other Light Beings, have joined together to assist humanity in its ascension process. There are a great number of us ready and available to counsel and work with you personally. The only fee we charge is your willingness to gain greater understanding of your evolutionary pathway, and your willingness to surrender your human ego to your Great God Self. Go with the flow of manifestations that will present themselves to you for your transformation and ascension.

I am El Morya now making myself available to you through my Diamond Heart of the Will of God.

Chapter Fifteen

Wake-Up Call from the Redwood Trees

We are the "Giants," the remnants of a very ancient civilization that most of you have long forgotten. The millennia have come and gone and we are still here, in gradually decreasing numbers at the hands of rapacious loggers whose only consideration is the amount of money they can make by reducing our population day by day.

As a species of the collective Devic Intelligence, our presence has graced this planet for millions of years, back to the time of the magical Land of Pan. For millions of years, the people of this planet have held us in great awe and respect for the beauty and wisdom we hold, and for the deep sense of peace and harmony we radiate far and wide from the surroundings where we abide. Those who have the ability to communicate and interact with us consciously receive our gifts and the knowledge we possess. Unknown to most of you, we have much knowledge and wisdom to share. Someday, you will wake up to this reality, and wish you had been more conscious of who we are and the important contributions we have made on your planet.

We lived and thrived on the ancient continent of Lemuria, far beyond this western shore.

At one time, our Spirit and physical form were spread

nearly everywhere on this planet. At this time, we are the
only survivors on the surface of the glory and beauty that
once was. We are the historians and a connecting link to
your ancestors, to your roots and your past-selves in the
Lemurian civilization and beyond. People have complained
again and again that Lemuria was lost without any trace.
We tell you that we are here, "unacknowledged." We are the
Ones who survived the cataclysmic changes that occurred
12,000 years ago, and we have remained on the Pacific Coast
for your benefit. Why have you not recognized us? Why do
you not appreciate the great service that we, as a species,
have offered to your planet for so very long, and the great
service we continue to provide to this very day, in spite of
the gradual and constant destruction of our species?

In the millions of years of service, no civilization has ever
sought to eliminate us so heartlessly and callously as twen-
tieth century Americans. We are being removed system-
atically by industrial giants with the full support of your
government. Governments are responsible for supporting
long-term benefits of the whole, not just the short-term
interests of lobbyists and exploiters. For the sake of a few
dollars you are eliminating your ancient heritage and destroying the Beings who are protecting you. You are, as the
analogy states, "the dogs that bite the hands of those who
feed and love them."

*Very few would ever have considered destroying
us the way you have today in this country. It
would have been considered an outrage and the
rape of one of Earth's most precious treasures.*

Always, in all regions and eras, we have been honored and
loved for the gifts from the Earth we were able to distribute
freely to all. The West Coast of the United States is now
what is left of ancient Lemuria's last treasures, and up until
about 60 years ago, thousands upon thousands of acres of
Redwoods graced and blessed the West Coast of this country.

Now there are only a few meager strips of us left here and there "for show." You are so far removed in your awareness from true beauty and value that very few of you have even noticed. Where have you been? What do you value?

***All our beauty is about gone, replaced by
a false sense of "progress" and much ugliness.***

Although most of us, as a species, have been destroyed by your modern technology and your lack of awareness and consideration, our Spirit continues to live. Every time one of us succumbs to the mechanical saw of a lumbermen, the Spirit of the dying tree moves on to another dimension for a new incarnation where it is loved, honored and appreciated. Our species, as a collective Devic Intelligence, also live in many higher dimensions of this planet and beyond, where we thrive and the inhabitants cherish our presence and our gifts. We live in great numbers inside the Earth and the subterranean cities of this planet where we grace the lives of the loving and wise beings who reside in those wondrous places.

You have so much to learn, my friends, of the "real values" of Life! If our words seem harsh to you, take them as a wake-up call, a plea for compassion for all other Life forms on this planet that are receiving the same harsh treatment from humanity. Ultimately, when you have reached a state of evolution high enough to understand the Eternal Laws of Oneness with all life, you will know that the love and compassion you accord to another, no matter what form it takes, is for your own benefit. As you trash the Earth and Her many kingdoms, ultimately, those energies will return to you. In your subsequent incarnations, you will become the recipients of your own destructive actions. This is cosmic law and it cannot be otherwise. The immutable laws governing this universe and all of Creation are always applied.

In all enlightened societies, no one ever cuts our bodies

for their personal use *(or profit)* until our incarnation is complete and the Spirit has departed from the form. It is only then that the wood is cut with great respect and skill, and used for multiple purposes. The wonderful wood we provide is one of the many gifts we offer the planet from our Spirit. It is not our purpose to be monopolized by a few profiteers and sold by multi-million dollar industrial corporations who hold no love or connection with Nature and Devic Evolution. We belong to all; no one group or individual has the right to "own us" and "dispose" of us as they please.

Stewardship of land and animals are major evolutionary initiations on the Path of Life.

Never can you claim to truly own a piece of land. By "Divine Rights" all land belongs to the body of your Earth Mother. She is sovereign. If you think you own a piece of land or rights to some land, you are only temporary stewards of that land. You are also totally accountable to the Higher Councils for what you do with it. In all enlightened societies, because wood is used wisely and judiciously, there is plenty for everyone and needs are supplied without any rationing or scarcity.

Have you ever noticed the difference in hurricane and tornado activity between the East Coast and the West Coast? Have you ever wondered why the West Coast is not subject to the same number of yearly cataclysms as occurs so frequently on the East Coast? It is our desire to tell you that the West Coast has been spared so many calamities each year because of "Our Presence." We are not "just trees" as you believe in your lack of spiritual consciousness; we are much more than that. Our tree form is just an outer shell housing our Great Spirit. Although our Spirit is incarnated in the form of giant trees, our collective Spirit is vast, powerful, all encompassing and wise, well beyond your present limited understanding and awareness.

156

We, the Redwood Trees, are mighty Guardians and Devas of the West Coast.

It is because of our presence there, our love and our great protective powers, that this country has been spared many calamities from Nature. Please be reminded that disasters from Nature are always caused by energetic imbalances in the Earth's energy grids, arising from vortexes of discordant energies created and accumulated by humanity. The misuse of creative energies, negative thinking, and lack of Love towards each other and other Life Forms create these vortexes.

We are the harmonizers of Nature where we live, and our influence radiates far and wide. Over the centuries, we have been able to absorb in our giant bodies much of your discordant energies, thus sparing the western hemisphere the consequences of many natural disasters.

When our numbers were greater near your shore and on your coast, we were much more effective at warding off potential disturbances or cataclysms from the Pacific Ocean or elsewhere. Now, with our numbers being so drastically reduced, be aware that our protection is equally reduced. This is our warning.

Our small numbers make it increasingly difficult for us to provide the West Coast with the much greater protection you will actually need in the very near future.

We would like to add that by steadily reducing our numbers, as you have for the last several decades, you are putting your shores, the western land of the U.S. and its inhabitants at much greater risk from cataclysmic disasters.

You are carelessly, without thought, destroying the guardians who have protected you, your shores and your land for eons of time.

157

Once we become extinct, we are not coming back to this dimension. We are going elsewhere to continue our service to life, to bless and radiate our purposes. The rest of us will join the millions of our species who have already departed. Our souls are immortal, as are yours.

The death of our bodies will become "a great loss" in this country as you will soon find out and a loss for the third dimension of this planet. If we cannot continue to do what we are here to do, we will move on to greener pastures where love, light and honor reigns and where we will be appreciated.

We are grateful to Aurelia Louise for taking the time to hear our call deep from within the recesses of her heart and soul, and for taking note of the urgent message we have been wanting to share with mankind for so long.

We have cradled you in our protection, love, wisdom, peace, harmony, beauty, wood and oxygen; we have adorned your landscape for millions of years throughout your many incarnations. You know us as we know you. Because of the fall to such a deep level of unconsciousness, you have forgotten your roots and your ancestry, and you have forgotten some of your best friends.

You no longer acknowledge the Earth as your Mother, an awesome Celestial, Living, Breathing Being of the highest order and intelligence, a Being that is loved, cherished and honored throughout all the planets of this solar system, the many galaxies of this universe and all other universes far beyond this one. She is the One who has supported unconditionally your personal evolution on Her body with such great Love, abundance and nurturing, for eons of time.

She has allowed you to damage, poison and destroy parts of Her body countless times in order to assist you in forging your evolutionary pathway. You have raped Her resources,

158

drained Her blood, the oil inside Her body, and killed and mutilated Her children.

Many of you are recklessly destroying large segments of land and the habitat of the many kingdoms that She also hosts on this planet besides humanity. You have been brutal to Her innocent ones from the animal kingdom and you have been brutal with each other. She considers all beings of Her many kingdoms as Her children, no matter what form they take. She loves all equally. You have forgotten that all kingdoms evolving on this planet, known or unknown to you, have equal rights to live here and share this planet, no matter what form they take.

Mankind was never given dominion over this planet to abuse and destroy other kingdoms, including ours.

The mandate mankind was given was to learn dominion over his own "lower nature," in order to return to his original divinity and innocence. We are sending you an "SOS" call today through this channel. Do what you can to preserve what is left of us. The time is now very close when you will need our protection more than ever before. If there are no longer enough of us to provide the protection you need during the imminent Earth changes at this time, you will have to ward off the consequences of your karmic creations without the added benefit of our protection. And then you will know! You will be calling on us in your soul, and it will be too late. Our Spirit will be living elsewhere, in the Lands of Love and Appreciation.

Our presence is indeed a great gift, something that is given only once to a planet. After millions of years of physical existence here in great numbers, with all the love we have offered to the Earth inhabitants and her many kingdoms, we have been brought to the brink of extinction by the heedlessness of one generation alone!

159

Once a planet loses the privilege of our presence through abuse, we do not return to that dimension.

We are the Spirit of Redwood Trees; we are loyal friends who have loved and cherished all of you for so very long. We are the Wise Giants who have cradled and nurtured all civilizations on your planet from the very beginning. We are Devas who hold Great Powers and Wisdom, and we are part of the Protection Team for this planet. We are the faithful servants of your blessed Earth Mother.

Chapter Sixteen

Telos, A Living Library

Greetings, my friends,

One of my names is Thomas, an elder of Telos. I came to live inside the mountain just days prior to the destruction of our continent. I was Aurelia's brother during her last life in Lemuria; she was my elder sister by several years. Because of the position of leadership she held at the time, she was very busy, but she always made time for me, always treating me with love and kindness; this is how I remember her.

It is my great pleasure to have the opportunity of being heard today on the surface of the Earth, to bring my energies to you with great love. Our time in Telos in the last 12,000 years has been very wondrous indeed on one hand, and on the other hand, we have felt the pain of separation from our family members living on the surface.

It is with great anticipation that we are preparing in our hearts, as soon as it is possible, to reunite with you more tangibly. But understand, my friends, it will not be in the third dimensional frequency as you now know it. You will have to meet us at least two-thirds of the way to the fifth dimension.

Our mission in Telos will not be accomplished fully until

we are all united again as one civilization. All the elders of Telos, basically the ones who have been communicating with you, have from time to time held a position on the Lemurian Council of Twelve and in the government of our city. But now, we have stepped back to allow the younger ones to hold these positions. We believe that everyone should be given an opportunity to hold the reins and experience the role of leadership under the guidance of the advisory committee of the elders.

Most of the elders of Telos have families that have increased tremendously in size. We have children, grandchildren, great grandchildren and additional generations who have never experienced your dimension physically. They are now becoming more and more curious to experience life on the surface. They honor your courage for having incarnated again and again into such difficult situations. So many of us, especially the younger ones, are now looking forward to the day when you will eliminate all violence. We wish, in our hearts and minds, to come out and assist you.

In Telos, one of my occupations is to be in charge of a vast library that contains crystal plates on which is recorded all of the history of the Lemurian culture, from the beginning to the end, and also all of what has transpired within and without the planet since the physical destruction of our continent. Our library also contains all the records of the "true" history of our planet of which surface humanity knows very little. I have a wonderful team working with me, quite large indeed, and we have been busy for quite some time duplicating all of our records in various languages, preparing for the time they will be made available to you to expand your knowledge and wisdom.

This is when, my beloveds, you will be able to access the true and wondrous history of your planet, of your Mother Earth and of the many civilizations which have lived here.

The complete and accurate history of your planet has never been known by your historians of the past 12,000 years. What you think you know is rather limited, and represents only distorted fragments of the true history. The real records will not be accessible until they are released. Many of your historians have done their best to write their own perceptions of Earth's history, but none of them was enlightened enough to accurately perceive or discern any segment of it, much less the whole story.

When you are permitted this kind of exploration, you will be able to access all of this information. We already smile, knowing that you will be surprised, astounded and stunned beyond measure.

Prior to the demise of Lemuria, all records were taken into Telos to be preserved for the knowledge and wisdom of future generations. We have a living library, not only for this planet, but also for the galaxy and this entire universe. We knew that very few records, if any, would survive the loss of the two major continents and the hardships that followed.

It is my perception that within the next 20 years or sooner, the duplicates of our entire record will be reintroduced to the surface for all of you to consult and study at your leisure. You will gain much wisdom from such extensive and accurate information. The technology to read these crystal plates will also be made available to you. Complete sets of these records will be made available to many parts of this planet. This is a huge task we undertake to organize for your benefit. Our work is a labor of love and it is with great joy that we perform this service to provide you access to the Earth's history in the not-too-distant future.

It is with great love that I embrace the three of you today *(Aurelia and two other ladies)*. You are truly part of the sisterhood of Telos on the inner plane. We regard you as such. There are many more of you on the surface who will be attracted to this material, who are also part of that sisterhood, whether you are conscious of it or not. I know that you have opened yourself to Adama, Ahnahmar, Galatia, Celestia and a few others you know in Telos. I now introduce myself and invite you to open yourself to me as well. I am eager and willing to reconnect with all of you, to assist you in increasing your joy and understanding. Until we meet again, I hold you very dear to my heart.

Chapter Seventeen

Final Words from Adama

I would like to conclude our messages by saying to all of you who are reading this material, it has been my honor and great pleasure to once again have a voice on the "surface" through the publishing of this information. I would also like to express my deep gratitude to Aurelia Louise for her persistent dedication to her mission, and for her vision of the impact her work will bring to all nations on this planet, blessing them with our energies and teachings. Such a great number of beloved souls everywhere are ready to open their hearts to their Lemurian heritage. May our books serve as the remembrance their souls need for the great and deep awakening they have been seeking.

We foresee that our teachings will travel far and wide to reach those who are connected with us worldwide, and will assist hundreds of thousands in their journey to spiritual freedom. I would like to assure all of you who will be reading our transmissions, wherever you are, that as you read, we will be with you at your side, sending you our love and encouraging you to open your heart and consciousness to greater and greater levels of awareness.

The energy that is transmitted to you through the words of our heart connection will change forever the perspective of your present life experience. Our intention throughout this book has been to give you a taste of what an enlightened civilization is like, and to encourage you to begin applying these principles as much as you can in your daily life. As you do, you will discover that your life will flow with greater ease and grace. All of you together, along with all of us from the Light Realm, will heal this planet. By cosmic law, we can only match your efforts. A few years from now, many of us will be walking among you to show you how to establish wondrous communities of Light, and lay the foundation for the new and permanent golden age on the surface of our planet.

Our emergence among you will create a heart-warming experience for all of you who await our return. Our presence on the "surface," mingling with you again as one civilization, is the reunion longed for by so many of you. I urge all of you to prepare the way for our coming. We are in total readiness to be among you now, but the readiness must also be created on your side. As it is, your world is not ready to receive our energies directly. I ask all of you, individually and collectively, to do whatever you can to first prepare yourself, and then spread the word with those who are ready to open up to this possibility.

Radiate your love and ask to be included *"on the list"* of those with whom we will make first contact. It does not matter where you live; we have ways of contacting anyone anywhere on the planet at the right moment. The requirements to be included *"on the list"* are that you first must desire it, open your consciousness to embrace your divinity, and then, be of service to self, to the planet and to your brothers and sisters living on it. Prepare the way for our emergence through your love and the sharing of your new truths. Remember that we will not meet you in your present level of consciousness. You must raise your vibration to at least two-thirds of the way to our dimension.

With these words, all of us in Telos join with me to send you blessings of love, healing, abundance, wisdom and divine grace. Know that we are the guides who can offer assistance at every step, just for the asking with the attunement of your heart to love and compassion.

I am your Lemurian Brother and Friend, Adama.

Regarding Channeling Adama
By Aurelia Louise Jones

At the present time, there are an increasing number of people claiming to be channeling Adama. On the Internet, all kinds of messages are floating around in his name. In some cases, I know these to be authentic, while others are not. Just because the name of Adama is written at the bottom of a message does not necessarily mean that it comes from him.

I take no responsibility for any information that is published by other people in the name of Adama or Ahnahmar; the information may or may not be authentic.

Since the Telos books, Volumes 1, 2 and 3 have been published, there are a surprising number of people who suddenly claim that they have become a new channel for Adama and for Ahnahmar. There are those who even claim they have become my replacement. All kinds of channeled information is now circulating on the Internet and else-where, especially in newsgroups, published in the name of Adama. Some are sweet and appear to be coming from the heart, while others are simply erroneous and do not carry the Lemurian vibration. Unfortunately, this is very confusing for serious truth seekers and for those who have not yet developed enough discernment and clarity to distinguish the difference between what is authentic and what is not.

Adama is often asked questions by people desiring to gain a level of discernment regarding channeled information written in his name. People want to know who they can trust and how to tell the difference between those who are truly channeling him and those who are simply channeling themselves or other entities of lesser vibration posing as Adama. It is not always easy, even for me, to discern who is authentic and who is not, or to judge the intentions of others, as judgments are always traps. Each person must exercise their own discernment, and thus gain their stripes in spiritual mastery.

Here is what Adama has to say:

For various reasons which must remain unknown to you, I would like to state that at this time I do not authorize anyone other than Aurelia Louise Jones to channel me officially with the intention of publishing books, or for participation in public presentations in my name. If this permission were granted indiscriminately, it would make it extremely difficult for those who have not yet attained the level of spiritual development necessary to discern which information is accurate and authentic, and which is not.

The risk of our teachings becoming distorted and biased once more, at the hands of those who have not yet received the initiations and inner training to bring forth our information would greatly increase. It would also create an invitation to those who have a personal agenda to corrupt our teachings again with non-truths, as they have done in the past. This is why our original teachings are no longer in existence; they have been corrupted again and again by those who do not have the clarity or integrity of intention these teachings require. We certainly do not want to see this happen again.

If our teachings that carry the Lemurian consciousness, which originally came from Divine Source, are permitted to be brought forth by too many people, these teachings may become distorted again, especially by those wanting to profit from a subject that has become popular. This would cause much confusion in the hearts and souls of those we are trying to reach, and those who are truly trying to reach us.

This is why for now, we are limiting ourselves to Aurelia who has a "pre-birth" contract to do this work with us. Those wanting to channel me without the proper preparation and without a specific invitation to do so, beyond offering the occasional message to a small group or to give comfort to someone in need, may be presenting an illusion, because I am not always present or willing to communicate.

If I am present at one of your gatherings, it does not mean that it is always appropriate for me to bring forth a message. We wish the hearts of those desiring communication to be in touch with the highest integrity of Lemurian energies, and not someone posing as Ahnahmar, myself or others from Telos.

According to Divine Law, it is the Master who chooses its channel and not the incarnated person. One must wait for an official invitation from a Master from the other side of the veil in order to channel that Master. No master is allowed to speak through a person unless this Master receives permission from the Creator Himself. The candidate to channel for a Master must have passed through spiritual initiations required by hierarchy over a period of several lifetimes to be granted such a privilege.

There are those who have used my image and have written sales pitches in my name to promote their products and their scams. Please know, dear ones, that I do not participate in such endeavors and that I am certainly not a salesman for those without integrity.

All channeled messages that are not authentic hold a vibration of personal agenda and can become spiritual traps. Be aware, my friends, that many of those who contributed to the destruction of both continents are also incarnated at this time, and some of them are determined to stop the Light from coming in. They want to stop the Lemurian emergence in any way they can. They will often disguise themselves as angels of Light coming to your rescue and make you all kinds of alluring offers. I ask you not to be deceived and always check with the discernment in your heart.

This time, my friends, the stakes are too high for the planet and for your own personal evolution. Be aware that you will all be confronted with tests of discernment in more ways than one. Do not buy into victim consciousness. Commit to becoming sovereign in your divine powers as masters.

Know that it is always my pleasure to connect and speak with you directly in your heart. Sometimes I am present in your gatherings radiating my energy and my love to all of you, but I remain silent and unnoticed. For us, the energy we bring is often more important to your transformation than the words. Many times words can be limiting. I ask you to receive and cherish these precious moments and hold what is shared deep within your heart. You do not have to broadcast on the Internet and elsewhere everything you receive from us. Most transmissions are directed and appropriate for those present at that time and not intended for public dissemination.

I also want to add that in Telos, I am the one who has volunteered to enter the public eye on the surface. The others, especially Ahnahmar, have not chosen to do so because their time has not yet come. Ahnahmar does not wish to have his image commercialized or go public other than in an occasional channeling here and there for Aurelia, the beloved of his heart, and for her writings.

Ahnahmar and I are certainly not interested in bringing forth messages through those beings who do not embody the integrity and transparency of the Lemurian vibration.

We are happy to give you personal messages when your heart tunes in to ours in your meditations. It is important that you learn to discern when those messages can be shared with others and when they should not be.

All messages from us, and from other beings of the light realms, always contain keys of wisdom you need to integrate for your advancement or to point the way to your next step on your pathway to self-realization. It is always more important to integrate fully what you have already received than to keep looking for the next message simply for the sake of accumulating more information to store in your mental body. Unless you integrate in your consciousness what you have already received, it becomes clutter in your mind that does not always serve you.

The Heart of Lemuria resides in each one of you, recognized or not. It is our sacred mission, along with Aurelia Louise Jones and those who work alongside her, to help you re-awaken to the totality of your divinity and the sacredness of your own journey.

Your willingness to open to energies that may stretch your understanding should never be threatened by feelings of insecurity. Therefore, we will continue to remind you to let what you hear and what you read be the truth within your own hearts where the only authenticity resides. Only with your hearts may you discern the many vibrations of the Divine, and determine which is most appropriate for you in the now moment.

Never hesitate to ask us for guidance in your heart. We will always answer. I am Adama, teacher for humanity.

Note from Aurelia Louise Jones

Every day I receive so much mail and internet communication from all over the world that it has become literally impossible for me to answer even a small percentage of this correspondence.

Please know that I read and appreciate your letters and wish that I could answer the hundreds of heartfelt communications I receive each week. All I can do while keeping up with my work is to send you all much love and appreciation. I ask for your compassion and understanding of my inability to answer you individually.

I am heartened by the ever-increasing momentum of the Lemurian Connection now reaching around the world. I bless you for the light you contribute to the awakening of humanity during this time of monumental change.

**For book information, Telos and
Lemurian Connection Associations,
see next three pages.**

Mount Shasta Light Publishing Publications

The Seven Sacred Flames $39.00

Seven Sacred Flames Prayer Booklet $7.00

Ascension Activation Booklet $7.00

Seven Sacred Flames Card Deck $16.00

Telos Book Series Card Deck $16.00

Telos – Volume 1 "Revelations of the New Lemuria".. $18.00

Telos – Volume 2 "Messages for the Enlightenment
   of a Humanity in Transformation" $18.00

Telos – Volume 3 "Protocols of the Fifth Dimension" . $20.00

The Effects of Recreational Drugs
   on Spiritual Development $4.00

Angelo's Message – "Angelo, the Angel Cat
   Speaks to all People on this Planet Regarding
   the Treatment of Animals by Humanity" $8.00

These publications can be purchased in the USA:

- Directly from us by phone or at our mailing address
- From our secure shopping cart on our web site:
  http://www.mslpublishing.com
- From Amazon.com
- Bookstores through New Leaf Book Distributing

If ordering by mail, CA residents, please include 8.25% sales tax. Also include shipping charges: Priority or Media mail, according to weight and distance.

Mount Shasta Light Publishing
P.O. Box 1509
Mount Shasta, CA 96067-1509 - USA
aurelia@mslpublishing.com
Phone: (Intl: 001) 530-926-4599
(If no answer, please leave a message)

Telos and Lemurian Connection Associations

Mission
The Telos World Wide Foundation has been established for the purpose of collaborating closely with Aurelia Louise Jones, Adama and the Lemurian teachings representing the Christ consciousness in its full application.

Telos USA
www.telos-usa.org
info@telos-usa.org
Also see: Lemurian Connection
www.lemurianconnection.com

Telos World-Wide Foundation, Inc.
E-mail: telos@telosinfo.org
Web Site: www.telosinfo.org

Telos Australia
www.telos-australia.com.au
robert@telos-australia.com.au
catherine@telos-australia.com.au

Telos-France
www.telos-france.com
telosfrance@me.com

Telos Europe
www.teloseurope.eu
telos-europe@me.com

Telos Finland
www.telosfinland.fi
telosfinland@me.com

Telos Japan
www.telos-japan.org
office@telos-japan.org

Canadian Distributors:

Telos World-Wide Foundation, Inc.
7400 St. Laurent, Office 326,
Montreal, QC - H2R 2Y1 – Canada
Phone: (001 Intl.) 1-514-940-7746
E-mail: telos@telosinfo.org
Web Site: www.telosinfo.org

For Canadian Bookstores:
Quanta Books Distributing
3251 Kennedy Road, Unit 20
Toronto, Ontario, MIV-2J0 - CANADA
Phone: 1-888-436-7962 or 416-410-9411
E-mail: quantamail@quanta.ca
Web: www.quanta.ca